FULLY
WHELMED

Library of Congress Cataloging-in-Publication Data

Includes bibliographical References

ISBN 978-1-7336998-2-2

Unless otherwise noted, Scripture quotations are
from the *Holy Bible: New International Version*®.
Copyright © 1973, 1978, 1984 by the International
Bible Society.

Scripture quotations marked ESV are from *The English
Standard Version*©2001 by Crossway Bibles, a division
of Good News Publishers.

Vertical Press Books

Cover design by Arrow Designs

Interior design by Olivier Darbonville

Editing and proofreading by Alli Mann and Leah Rezin

FULLY
WHELMED

SHIFTING FROM
OVERWHELM
to
OVERFLOW

LISA DETTINGER

VERTICAL PRESS BOOKS

Acknowledgments

Thank you, Jesus, for loving me through my overwhelm and into your overflow.

You are my Life.

Thank you, Travis, for being an earthly example of how Christ loves His church.

You are my hero.

Thank you, Zac, Abi, and Gabe, for your grace and support.

You are my most precious fruit.

Thank you, John Diaz de Leon, Alisha Stafford*, Sondra Corbett-Wood, Sharon Smith*, Joel Baraka, Anne Hogan, Kelly Girard*, Andrea Fox*, PeggyAnn Poss, and Dugan Sherbondy, for your authentic contributions to this book.

You are my inspiration.

Thank you, Leah Rezin and Alli Mann, for your editing skills and insightful suggestions.

You are my buttresses.

Thank you, family and friends, for your eagerness to see this book come to fruition.

You are my encouragement.

*Names have been changed.

Contents

CHAPTER ONE

Heavenly Headlines

I've been praying for you. Yes, *you*. Besides God, nobody really knows what you're going through: how much you're juggling, what you've been through, what you're facing. And since it's just the two of us here, we can be gut-level honest, so go ahead and relax your shoulders, take a deep breath, and let your guard down. I won't judge.

Are you overwhelmed?

Maybe you have had it "up to here" with your kids. You love them, of course, but they are driving you crazy. Maybe you're drowning in mounting bills and don't see a way out. Perhaps you received a dreaded diagnosis and now you're in for a battle to survive. Holiday season? "Stressmas" is a better word for it. Maybe it's your marriage. Why does it have to be so difficult? Why can't your husband be more like so-and-so's? Or maybe you're grieving over the death of a loved one. There's a gaping hole in your heart that will never be filled and no one understands why you're not over it yet. Maybe that mile-long to-do list just keeps. Getting. Longer. Or you hear your father or mother's voice continually ringing in your ears that you'll never be good enough.

Maybe it's all these things at the same time. When it rains it pours, right? You seem to be the one that *everything* happens to. So your life constantly hovers between overwhelm and numbness. You're either teetering on the edge of a breakdown or you're numb to it all because you've got to cope somehow. Not feeling anything is a safer alternative to feeling everything.

Maybe it's none of those things. You've got it pretty good relatively speaking. Life is busy and somehow you manage it all. But it doesn't take much to get you anxious and worried, so when there's a kink in the chain of how things are *supposed* to look it requires your full attention to make sure everything gets back to normal again – whatever "normal" means. Keeping everyone happy and everything under control is exhausting though. It can be downright overwhelming.

Friend, receive a hug through these pages. Like I said, I've been praying for you – for every person who reads this book, actually. And because I love you I'm going to be gut-level honest with you.

You choose your overwhelm.

Sounds harsh, doesn't it? Who do I think I am, telling you that? After all, I admitted in the very first paragraph that I don't know exactly what you're going through. You probably want to throw this book down and condemn it (and me). I understand.

But hear me out. I've been overwhelmed by my circumstances too. Sometimes I've handled it with grace and other times, well... not so much. Sometimes I've felt utterly defeated and hopeless. Like when I lost my baby during the second trimester (the alleged "safe" time).

I got to relive the experience multiple times. If you would have told me I could "choose my overwhelm" during that season I probably would have glared ice shards into you before stomping away in utter contempt.

But I needed to hear it.

I needed someone to tell me that God isn't cruel, that He didn't kill my baby, that *I* didn't kill my baby, and that He wasn't trying to punish me for my past sins. Those thoughts kept me in defeat and bitterness for a long time. I needed to know I had a choice between being defeated by my overwhelm and *surrendering* my overwhelm.

So because we're being gut-level honest, I'll share how I, a Bible-believing, sold-out-for-Jesus Christian, handled my overwhelm.

AN OVERWHELMING EXPERIENCE

It was my first year teaching. I was ecstatic to be pregnant and being midtrimester, knew I'd have to let the cat out of the bag with my boss and colleagues before my belly bump got much bigger.

And then I lost my baby. It was devastating. Even though the doctors examined me multiple times and kept saying there was nothing left, I got to relive the experience of losing this much-wanted baby over and over. It was like being shot in the gut repeatedly even though the first shot was already fatal.

After being reassured that *this* time I was all clear, I got back into the routine of teaching. Then, in the middle of a class, I suddenly *had to* run to the bathroom. As I was fumbling in vain to find something to sop the scarlet mess, there was a blaring announcement over the loud speaker calling for an immediate evacuation of the entire school. "Please do not stop to collect your backpack, purse, or anything else. Simply proceed *immediately* out of the building and go to your fire drill stations on the field." Turns out it was a bomb threat. While I'm dealing with miscarriage mess. In white shorts.

This was *the* craziest timing ever! I thought I was done with all that after the fiasco during my very first PTA night when I had to excuse myself for the same reason. The medical community had told me (more than once) that my miscarriage was officially over – and yet here I was reliving it again!

Anger, fear, sadness, and urgency swept over me like a tidal wave as I scrambled to put myself together with a bunch of rolled up TP so I could rush outside before the building exploded. (It didn't.) *Might as well take me with it, Lord. This is unbelievable timing! Why me? Why now?* I found my students with my teacher's aide and then scanned the staff for anyone pre-menopausal who might have some supplies for me. I explained the situation calmly and discreetly (read: quietly hyperventilating in humiliated desperation) to a handful of women, but to no avail.

At this point I was ready to throw a full-blast tantrum. Have you ever wanted to throw an adult tantrum? I imagined myself jumping, screaming, flailing my arms and crying and then dropping to the ground so I could slam my fists into it and promulgate the unfairness of this moment.

Instead, I took the advice of a couple teachers and headed across the street to a row of businesses. Yes, I went door-to-door begging business owners for feminine hygiene products. Can you imagine?

"Excuse me, ma'am, but I'm a teacher over there at Lincoln and we're in the middle of an evacuation for a bomb threat." (Gulp.) "I'm having complications with a miscarriage and I'm wondering if you have any feminine hygiene products."

"No, I'm sorry. I can't help you."

"Try the grocery store."

"Uh, no. This is a *men's* barber shop."

I gingerly waddled back to the school grounds, which were still occupied by the entire school. Wiping away escaped tears, I struggled to regain my composure before my face could be seen by the staff and students. I could tell by their glances the entire staff knew my plight, but they were helpless. My anger at this injustice was tempered only by my deep humiliation.

What the h--- God! It's bad enough I'm dealing with the death of the baby I so desperately wanted, but now I have to deal with all this on top of it? All the garbage with my stupid infertile body leading up to this pregnancy, already experiencing this loss twice, and now I've got this? What am I supposed to do here? *&%*#!! Fat lotta good it does to worship a God Who doesn't show even a modicum of compassion!

You should know, I rarely swear. And my emotions up to that point had been fairly stable. Have you ever felt so flabbergasted by your circumstances that you did or said things you didn't realize could even come out of you? Uh huh. Me too. Obviously. I imagined newspapers in Heaven with the headline, "So-called Christian Woman Swears, Cries, Throws Tantrum."

I approached my boss, the 60-something *male* principal of the school. I had been hiding my pregnancy so he had no idea what was coming.

"Uh. Umm. Mr. Arnold, sir. I know this is a bad time, but… I'mhavingamisscarriagerightnowandIcan'tdoanythingaboutitandI don'tknowwhattodocuzIdon'thavemykeysorpurseoranything."

At this point I took a breath and glanced up at his face just as it transformed from surprise to concern. He reached into his pocket, grabbed his car keys and said, "Here, take my car and go where you need to go and do what you need to do."

Oh, thank you Jesus for that man (and the fact that he kept his car keys in his pocket)!

My gratitude was short-lived. Have you ever tried driving without actually sitting down? There was no way I was going to defile his car. My grandparents lived in an assisted living facility near the school where I taught so I drove there and called my midwife. I was hysterical but didn't want to scare my grandparents by letting out a blood-curdling scream, so I dialed the number with my hands shaking and jaw tight as I tried unsuccessfully to hold it all together.

"Lisa, now take a deep breath. I'm going to meet you at the hospital. Can Travis get you there? You're going to need a D & C, honey."

My unmet-need-for-tantrum anger and "suck it up buttercup, the school's watching" efforts gave way to a sense of utter defeat and fear. *Another procedure? Surgery? Another invasion of the womb that was meant to nourish and protect my baby? Why does it have to be this difficult, Lord? Why do I need to keep reliving this with each experience being worse than the last?*

I was a basketcase at this point, so she prescribed valium.

I've never done drugs, but I ingested the valium she prescribed and begged for more. Again, I envisioned a headline in Heaven: "So-called Christian Woman Willingly Takes Mind-Altering Drug and Requests More." I didn't care. Have you ever felt so overwhelmed that you didn't care? I just wanted this whole experience to go away, Heavenly headlines or not.

In the surgical prep room with the anesthesiologist, I began trembling from deep within, like a volcano threatening to erupt. I was overwhelmed with fear, disbelief, disappointment, anger, loneliness, and frustration. I felt defeated and hopeless in that moment. Would my body ever be able to carry a baby to term? Or even get pregnant again? Will this procedure hurt as bad as my heart? Does God care?

I peeled my eyes off the wallpaper border that lined the top of the walls with watermelons (classic early 90's). Turning my head to the left, I looked resolutely into the eyes of the anesthesiologist as he prepared my veins and said, "Toast me."

True story. And that's just one example of me being overwhelmed by my circumstances. Heck, I've had whole seasons of overwhelm: from relationships, kids, finances, my body, weighty responsibilities, harassment, identity crises, people who were seemingly "out to get" me, a too-busy schedule, and on and on...

Okay, let's get back to that "you can choose your overwhelm" thing. I certainly didn't choose to lose my baby or to relive the experience multiple times. I didn't choose to have a bomb threat while I experienced it either. And later, I didn't choose to have our seemingly insurmountable non-insurance-covered medical bills that referred to our baby as a "product of conception" and a "spontaneous abortion" – words that cut like a knife. Frankly, I didn't feel like I had a choice in any of it.

CHOOSING DEFEATED OR SURRENDERED

However, there's a difference between defeated overwhelm and surrendered overwhelm. I was in defeated overwhelm during that season and it lasted for months while we also experienced infertility. I didn't realize I could choose a different perspective.

Defeated overwhelm feels like being inside a too-small animal trap that only has locks on the *outside* and there is no hope for escape. The feeling sometimes comes suddenly with a traumatic event, conversation, or realization. At other times defeated overwhelm sneaks up on us. Things that start with excitement gradually become burdensome. Sometimes overwhelm occurs after a "series of unfortunate events" that leave us feeling like a deflated punching bag.

Surrendered overwhelm is an acknowledgment that our circumstances are more than we can handle on our own. Yet in the midst of it all, there is an inexplicable inner peace knowing that the One Who loves us enough to die for us provides hope because He also *conquered* death for us (Jesus, our Living hope!).

We don't trust what's happening around us, but we trust Him because He is with us in our circumstances. More than that, He is *in* us. So ultimately, when our situation feels overwhelming, it is His Presence that can whelm from within us. We can surrender it to Him.

That was not how I experienced losing my baby.

My miscarriage story is an example of what defeated overwhelm often looks like: messy, chaotic, humiliating, untimely, emotionally charged, hopeless, helpless, and seemingly never-ending.

Like losing a much-wanted baby, living in a state of overwhelm is like siphoning any sense of control. The life within that was intended for joy drains out of us. Our interactions with people become a transaction of desperation rather than a true connection.

We might try to run away from the feeling of overwhelm by buffering with drugs, alcohol, food, or some other distraction. We get angry because life's unfair and there's nothing we can do about it. In our anger, we say and do things that are counter to how we are *supposed* to behave according to whatever environment we're in.

In an attempt to control the situation we become exhausted until finally, at our wit's end, we admit we can't handle it and either begrudgingly ask for help, explode, or curl up into a ball and shut everyone and everything out. We feel like the whole world is watching us drain away and we can't find the tangible protection we need to stop the bleeding.

Or maybe that was just me.

But I doubt it.

AN INVITATION

Let's journey together to shift from a defeated overwhelm to a surrendered overwhelm that gives way to a peaceful and joyful overflow, from being overwhelmed by messy and depressing circumstances to overflowing with Life abundant - regardless of our circumstances. You've already shown you would choose overflow *if you could* because you're reading this book.

You *can*.

Welcome to a journey where you can choose to shift your perspective, where you can give yourself permission to experience the human emotions of your overwhelming circumstances while simultaneously experiencing the Presence of the Living God whelming you from within, causing you to overflow with Him.

You'll be reading testimonies throughout the book from brothers and sisters in Christ who have gone through the fire and they *do not smell like smoke*. Some of them continue to experience the scorching heat of their overwhelming circumstances, yet they have tasted and seen that the Lord is good (Psalm 34:8) and they are fully whelmed.

You'll have an opportunity to reflect after each chapter and to allow the Holy Spirit to transform you by renewing your mind (Romans 12:2). I invite you to grab a journal and maybe even a friend to help you process the questions. I will too.

We'll get up-close and personal. I won't be holding anything back.

Let's do this.

For Reflection and Regeneration

1. Consider a time when you were in a state of defeated (hopeless) overwhelm in the past.

   a. What was the circumstance?

   b. What would the hypothetical headlines in Heaven say about you in the midst of that overwhelming circumstance?

   c. What "fixed" your overwhelm, if anything?

   d. Did your "fix" happen in your circumstances or in what happened inside you?

2. How often do you feel overwhelmed?

3. Do you feel good about how you currently handle overwhelm?

   a. Do you consider it defeated or surrendered overwhelm?

   b. What are you telling yourself in your overwhelm?

4. Do you want the people you care about the most to handle overwhelm the same way you do? Why or why not?

5. How do you *want* to handle circumstances that could overwhelm you?

6. Spend time in prayer. Ask the Lord how He feels about your overwhelm.

CHAPTER TWO

I AM in Three Circles

Grab a cup of coffee and nestle in. We're going to get to the heart of who we are because that is the foundation for how we think, speak, and act. What we believe about Who God is and how He sees us determines how we think about our circumstances.

"Identity" is quite the buzzword these days. Many religious organizations have convinced us we're sinners who *should* do this and *shouldn't* do that in order to be acceptable in the eyes of pious church-goers. They postulate we're destined to remain "Sinners in the Hands of an Angry God."

We believers don't want God angry with us so we'll try really hard to be good Christians despite our sinful selves. We plaster a smile on our faces, perform our Christian "should-dos" with as much self-deprecation as possible to be considered humble, and continue our daily lives as helpless, hopeless sinners.

To combat our feelings of guilt and performance anxiety, some of us seek self-help books and repeat meaningless mantras while our souls continue to wither in the stifling negativity of our alleged identity. We learn to speak affirmations (Stuart Smalley anyone?) and blah, blah, blah...

Or we respond by listening to feel-good pastors tell us the "three simple steps to a better marriage." So we do and do and do what they say and get worn out from trying so hard. Or maybe we give up trying and accept our fate of being hopeless sinners with a God Who is sometimes happy with us and sometimes not, depending on how often we read our Bible and how well we follow the rules that day.

It's all sheer absurdity.

WHERE IDENTITY BEGINS

Our identity doesn't start with DO or NOT DO. It starts with BE. Who is your BE? In other words, who are you at your very core? Are you a sinner or are you a saint? Your answer to this question bears consequences for how you handle overwhelm: defeated by circumstances you can't control *or* surrendered, trusting in and walking with the One Who loves you abundantly in all circumstances.

Who does *God* say we are? He should know, since He created us! Several years ago a friend challenged me to ask God that very question. She said, "Ask God, 'Who do You say that I am?'" I planned to broach the subject with Him the next morning. I needed to gear up for this kind of confrontation with the Almighty. Would I hear from Him? Would I like what I heard? I decided before drifting to sleep that He'd probably tell me I'm a sinner saved by grace. More on this later...

To know who we are we must first know Who *He* is.

God *wants* us to know who He is. Check out the verses below (bolded by me).

When Abram was ninety-nine years old, the LORD appeared to him and said, ***"I am God Almighty*** *; walk before me and be blameless.." Genesis 17:1*

"I am the God of your father*, Abraham," He said. "Do not be afraid, for I am with you and will bless you." Genesis 26:24*

"I Am Who I Am. Say this to the people of Israel: I Am has sent me to you." Exodus 3:14

"I am the Lord who heals you." Exodus 15:26

"I am the Lord your God, who rescued you from the land of Egypt, the place of your slavery." Exodus 20:2

"Be still, and know that I am God! I will be honored by every nation. I will be honored throughout the world." Psalm 46:10

"Don't be afraid, for I am with you. Don't be discouraged, for I am your God. I will strengthen you and help you. I will hold you up with my victorious right hand." Isaiah 41:10

"I am the Lord; that is my name! I will not give my glory to anyone else, nor share my praise with carved idols." Isaiah 42:8

"I, yes I am the Lord, and there is no other Savior. First I predicted your rescue, then I saved you and proclaimed it to the world. No foreign god has ever done this. You are witnesses that I am the only God," says the Lord. Isaiah 43:11-12

"From eternity to eternity I am God. No one can snatch anyone out of my hand. No one can undo what I have done." Isaiah 43:13

This is what the Lord says— your Redeemer and Creator: "I am the Lord, who made all things. I alone stretched out the heavens. Who was with me when I made the earth?" Isaiah 44:24

"Remember the things I have done in the past. For I alone am God! I am God, and there is none like me." Isaiah 46:9

"For I am the Lord! If I say it, it will happen." Ezekiel 12:25

"I am the Lord, and I do not change." Malachi 3:6

Jesus answered, "I am. And in the future, you will see the Son of Man sitting at the right hand of God, the Powerful One, and coming on clouds in the sky." Mark 14:62

*Then Jesus said, "**I am He [the Messiah]**—I, the one talking to you."* John 4:26

*Jesus answered, "I tell you the truth, before Abraham was even born, **I am!**"* John 8:58

*Jesus said to her, "**I am the resurrection and the life**. Those who believe in me will have life even if they die."* John 11:25

*Jesus answered, "**I am the way, and the truth, and the life**. The only way to the Father is through me."* John 14:6

*"Believe me when I say that **I am in the Father and the Father is in me**. Or believe because of the miracles I have done."* John 14:11

*The Lord God says, "**I am the Alpha and the Omega. I am the One who is and was and is coming. I am the Almighty**."* Revelation 1:8

Those verses demonstrate that God wants His BE known - His "I AM." His identity. Once that's established, we can better understand who *we* are. When we begin to see how truly awesome He is and how much He loves us, we can overflow regardless of our circumstances.

We know from Scripture that God's I AM is a Trinity. He is made of three persons: the Father, the Holy Spirit, and the Son. (See Matthew 28:19, Luke 3:22, John 14:26, John 15:26, Acts 2:33, Acts 10:38, 2 Cor. 13:14, Gal. 4:6, Eph. 1:17, Eph. 2:18, Eph. 2:22, Heb. 4:12-13, Heb. 9:14, 1 Peter 1:2, 1 Cor. 12:4-6, Eph. 4:4-6, and Jude 20:21.) Jesus was *begotten* of the Father *through* the Holy Spirit (Luke 1:35). We can think of the Trinity, the Three-in-One, like a diagram of three circles, each wrapped within the next. The circles are three in one like God is three in one.

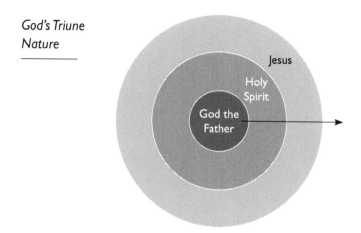

God's Triune Nature

The Bible tells us we are made in the image of God. (See Gen 1:26-28, Gen. 5:1-2, Gen. 9:6, Rom. 8:29, and James 3:9.) That means we are also a trinity. (Isn't that so cool?) We have a spirit, a soul, and a body, and each of these corresponds to God's image.

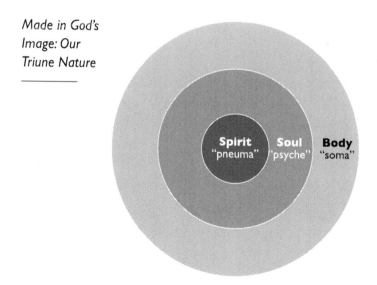

Made in God's Image: Our Triune Nature

Our spirit ("pneuma") is the very core of our being like God the Father is the core of the Trinity.

Our soul ("psyche") is the second layer in the circle and represents our thoughts, emotions, will, and personalities. This corresponds with the Holy Spirit ring of the Trinity.

Our body ("soma") is the outer layer of the circle and corresponds with the "Jesus" part of the Trinity in that He was God in the flesh. (See Col 1:15-16, Col. 2:9-10, John 1:1-2, John 1:14, Phil. 2:5-11, Matt. 1:23, and Heb. 1:2-3.)

In Hebrews 4:12, we read about the distinctions between the spirit, soul, and body ("joints and marrow").

For the word of God is living and active, sharper than any two-edged sword, piercing to the division of soul and of spirit, of joints and of marrow, and discerning the thoughts and intentions of the heart.

The "thoughts and intentions of the heart" represent being motivated from the outside in (having the mind set on things of the flesh) or being motivated from the inner spirit outward (having the mind set on the Spirit).

Those who live according to the flesh have their minds set on what the flesh desires; but those who live in accordance with the Spirit have their minds set on what the Spirit desires. Romans 8:5

How is it possible that even though we were created in God's image we can have our minds set on what the flesh desires - being motivated from the outside in?

HOW WE BECAME "OUTSIDE IN"

In the Garden of Eden, Adam and Eve enjoyed the freedom of eating fruit from all the trees in the garden except one - the Tree of the Knowledge of Good and Evil. (That meant they could eat of the

Tree of Life, though we don't read whether they did or not before the fall. What would *that* fruit taste like?)

Enter: the serpent. We know the story. The bottom line is that Adam and Eve chose to listen to and believe a source *outside* their Creator. The enemy presented a new perspective that appealed to their pride, which led to their disobedience, which led to the death of their spirits, the baggage in their souls, and the aging and death of their bodies.

We inherited that sinful condition, which includes taking in information about ourselves, God, and the world from a source *other* than God Himself. We inherited the inevitable death of our body! We are born into a state of spiritual identity theft (spiritual emptiness) and until we know Christ, we define ourselves by our circumstances (what people say to or about us, our environment, our financial status, what we do or don't have, what happens to us…).

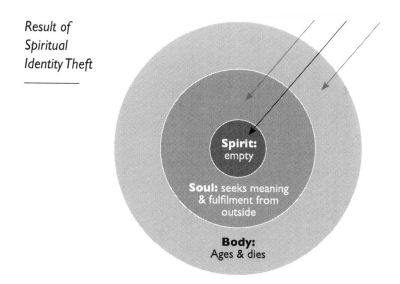

Result of Spiritual Identity Theft

Spirit: empty

Soul: seeks meaning & fulfilment from outside

Body: Ages & dies

But wait!!! Here comes the best news ever. When we come to know Jesus Christ as our Lord and Savior, our inner spirit shifts from empty to full of Life! (See 2 Cor. 5:17, Jn 3:3-7, Rom. 8:9, 2 Peter 1:4, 1 Cor.

3:16-17, Eph. 2:1-5, and Eph. 5:8.) Wow! We get to have God's Spirit living inside us; a new nature with a new identity. Incredible!

New Nature
in Christ
_____

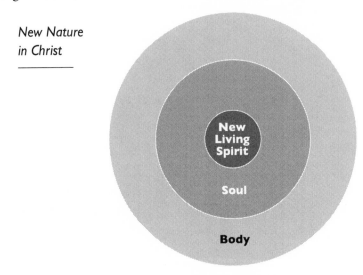

Here are a few different translations of 2 Corinthians 5:17 that are fun to chew on.

New Living Translation
This means that anyone who belongs to Christ has become a new person. The old life is gone; a new life has begun!

English Standard Version
Therefore, if anyone is in Christ, he is a new creation. The old has passed away; behold, the new has come.

New International Version
Therefore, if anyone is in Christ, the new creation has come: The old has gone, the new is here!

Good News Translation
Anyone who is joined to Christ is a new being; the old is gone, the new has come.

The Passion Translation
Now, if anyone is enfolded into Christ, he has become an entirely new creation. All that is related to the old order has vanished. Behold, everything is fresh and new.

King James Bible
Therefore if any man be in Christ, he is a new creature: old things are passed away; behold, all things are become new.

According to that verse, when we are in Christ, we are made new. Our Spirit becomes alive with God's Presence! We are even called God's temple in 1 Cor. 3:16, 2 Cor. 6:16, Eph. 2:22, and 1 Pet. 2:5. Now *that's* good news. Heck, in the Old Testament, people would die if they got too close to the Presence of the Lord and now we can have His Presence inside us! Amazing!

GOD-GIVEN IDENTITY

Okay, let's get back to my burning question for God. ("Who do You say I am?") It was my morning devotional time and I prepared Him for my question (even though I realized He never actually needs "preparing"). "Okay, Lord, I'm going to ask you now. Ready?" (Pause. Deep breath.) "Who do You say that I am?" Suddenly, one word washed over me like a warm shower:

"Beloved."

Not just loved, but *be*loved. The word implies more than a conditional love from afar. I could almost picture Jesus gathering me into His arms. That word was so unexpected, I knew it must have been the Holy Spirit.

After revelling in that for a few moments, I realized the contrast between how I saw myself (as a sinner) and how the Lord saw me as His new creation (a saint). I began to realize that the inner core of my being, because it contains the very Spirit of God, is saintly! It's good! It's beloved to Him! *I* am beloved to Him!

But I'm not perfect like Him. I'm still capable of sinning. Here's the thing: when we become born again as a new creation in Christ, our inner core (our spirit) is indeed all new. However, that second ring that includes our thoughts, emotions, memories, and personality does *not* become completely new at that instant.

That soul ring of the three circles is where the battle takes place, and that's why we're called to "be transformed by the renewing of our minds" (Romans 12:2). Overwhelm happens in the soul. When we are defeated by it, we are living from the outside in. When we are surrendered, we are living from the inside out.

When we look to *outside sources* for joy, peace, and fulfillment, we are doing the same thing Adam and Eve did when they fell into sin. When we look to the One True Source to define us, acknowledging that because of Jesus we can become a temple for the Holy Spirit to reside, we can find joy, peace, and fulfillment in any circumstance.

We're still capable of sin in our old patterns of thinking and in our old habits (which take place in our soul), but our very core is "saint" not "sinner." When we sin it's a case of mistaking our identity from our "old man" (old thinking patterns) instead of embracing our "new man" (new creation in Christ in the core of our being).

We are now faced with a choice. We can perceive God, ourselves, and the world through our circumstances (which are *outside* our inner circle), or we can perceive God, ourselves, and the world through the Holy Spirit, Who resides in our inner core. Are you looking to your circumstances (family, friends, job, finances, health…) to define you - to give you your identity - or are you looking to your Creator Who makes all things new (including us)?

You are His beloved. When you experience this revelation, His love can become more overwhelming to you than your circumstances. It will whelm you from your inner core, radiate through your three circles, and overflow onto others.

For Reflection and Regeneration

1. Do you identify more with being a sinner or with being a saint? Why?

2. Imagine being face to face with Jesus. What do you see in His eyes?

3. Still face to face with Jesus, what does He see in *your* eyes?

4. Read 2 Peter 1:1. Who is Peter writing to?

5. Read 2 Peter 1:3. What has His divine power given us?

   a. Is the verse referring to something that will be given in the future or has it *already* been given to us?

6. Read Ephesians 1:15-23.

   a. What is Paul praying for in verse 17 and in verse 18?

   b. In verses 19 and 20, what is "the incomparably great power for us who believe" the same as?

7. When you feel (or have felt) overwhelmed by your circumstances, is that feeling coming from your spirit ("pneuma," alive in Holy Spirit) or your soul ("psyche," thoughts and feelings)?

8. Spend time in prayer. Ask God to reveal His "I AM" to you. Ruminate on that for awhile. Ask Him, "Who do you say that I am?"

CHAPTER THREE

Whelmed

If overwhelmed means I've got more on my plate than what I think I can handle, then what does "whelmed" mean? I'm filled to the brim? *Almost* overwhelmed? That doesn't sound too fun either. Allow me to put my teacher hat on as we unpack these words.

According to the Oxford Dictionary, **over**whelm means "to bury or drown beneath a huge mass; to defeat completely; to give too much of a thing to (someone); inundate." Yup, been there, felt that. Oxford says **under**whelm means "fail to impress or make a positive impact on (someone); disappoint." Okay, we've all had moments of underwhelm (ho-hum) too. So what is "whelmed?"

Apparently, contemporary writers often use "whelm" to indicate a middle stage between underwhelm and overwhelm. However, according to Merriam-Webster associate editor Kory Stamper, "whelm," a word that dates back to the 1300's, originally meant to capsize something or to overturn. Further research reveals a deeper perspective on the word "whelmed." Lexico.com provides three definitions for it:

1. Verb: engulf, submerge, or bury
   A swimmer whelmed in a raging storm.

2. Verb: well up or flow
   The brook whelmed up from its source.

3. Noun: an act or instance of flowing or heaping up abundantly;
   a surge
   The whelm of the tide...

Note: Stamper's fourteenth century version of the word implies that something or someone is acting on an object to capsize it (whelm it). Lexico's definitions imply that the object itself is doing the whelming. The second two definitions are especially noteworthy. Imagine a brook "whelming up from its source" and picture a "whelm of the tide."

When we're overwhelmed, we're being submerged, buried, or defeated *by* something. When we're whelmed, we are welling up, flowing, heaping up abundantly, or surging. Here's what that looks like with the concept of the three circles.

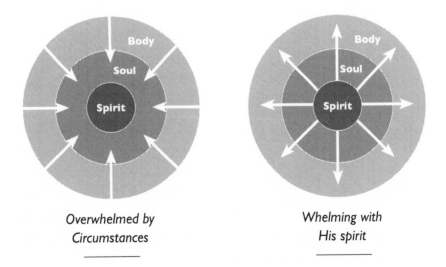

Overwhelmed by   *Whelming with*
Circumstances   *His spirit*

FROM SWAMPED TO WHELMED

Time to walk down my memory lane for an illustration. Around age 12 I decided to take canoe lessons while at a YMCA summer camp. I wasn't a strong swimmer, so learning to skillfully glide on *top* of the water appealed to me.

Everything was going swimmingly (hah!) until I found out we were going to swamp our canoe. My buddy and I were to fill the canoe with water, capsize it, get underneath it, then push it up out of the water while flipping it to its upright position.

Huh?

Once upright, we were to swim to opposite edges of the canoe and drag our bodies across the top to get back in.

Knowing I was about to do all this induced a roiling of my innards.

Had I known this was coming, I would have signed up for crafts (which *under*whelm me, to say the least). In my mind, the point of canoe lessons was to stay on *top* of the water, not sink the canoe and get under it!

Thank God we were required to wear life jackets. As I prepared to face my doom, my fumbling fingers fastened the life jacket as tightly as possible while I plastered a fake smile on my face and tried to look nonchalant. I'd be so embarrassed if anyone else knew I was internally freaking out.

We paddled out into the water with our instructors a good distance away. Next we rocked the canoe back and forth until water began to flood the sides. This was so counterintuitive! I tightened my clenched fists and stiffened my arms in an attempt to stop the rocking, deciding this was really *not* a good idea and we should stop.

It was too late. My canoe buddy, oblivious to my plight, continued fiercely rocking the canoe as the water overwhelmed our vessel. There was nothing I could do to stop it.

My arms returned to their spaghetti state and I white-knuckled the sides of the canoe in sheer desperation, my heart nearly pounding out of my tightly-clasped life jacket.

It happened in slow motion: the canoe began to tip onto one side and my buddy and I slid out of it and into the lake. There we were, floating on the water with our overturned canoe a couple yards away (AKA our "whelmed" canoe, according to 1300's English).

A flicker of pride washed over me as I realized we had, in fact, swamped our canoe.

In the next moment I realized with claustrophobic anxiety that we still needed to put ourselves under that beast to force it upright again and return to my much happier place - on *top* of the water.

We lifted the side of the canoe just enough to duck our heads under it and at that moment I felt the bottom of the lake under my feet. Turns out we weren't in over our heads after all! The water was about shoulder-deep.

My buddy and I stood facing each other in silence under the metal roof. I couldn't see much, but I heard the shallow echoing of our breathing bouncing off the metal and I felt the stillness - the peacefulness - of our little shelter. The rest of the world existed apart from this moment and I decided I felt safe there. We had whelmed our canoe and for about 10 seconds rested peacefully under it, grinning from ear to ear.

Suddenly, inspiration whelmed inside *me* and I knew beyond a shadow of a doubt this canoe was going upright again. The words came out of my mouth unexpectedly: "On the count of three - on my left and your right! One... two... three!" The canoe obediently flipped upright and we each swam to opposite sides at opposite ends, bracing ourselves to clamber aboard.

The hands that white-knuckled the edges of the canoe a few minutes ago now resolutely gripped these same edges with a new boldness. Make no mistake about it, sliding back onto this now-tamed beast belly-down and legs flailing was not graceful. It was awkward and strategic.

And successful.

Once onboard, we cheered with delight and began our celebratory journey back to shore. I felt like I had conquered the world. If I could swamp a canoe and come back to shore victorious once, surely I could do it again. Swamp shwamp.

WHEN THE WATER COMES IN

We all have different levels of overwhelm. Some of us know our canoe can hold a great deal of water before it becomes overwhelmed. Others of us begin anticipating overwhelm with just a few splashes of water. Or before we've even gotten into the canoe.

Regardless of our capacity, we see the water rising and feel as though there's nothing we can do about it. Our canoe is being overwhelmed. This is where we get to choose to be defeated or surrendered in our overwhelm.

If we start to feel the canoe sinking from the onslaught of rushing water (we feel the stress, strain, sorrow, or anxiety becoming more than we think we can handle), we can hopelessly sink with it (allow it to bring us down completely) or we can intentionally get into the water, find the intimately whispering peace that God offers, and *whelm* (experience a surge rising up from us).

Staying in defeated overwhelm is just as hopeless and helpless as believing we're sinners at our core. We are not hopeless and helpless sinners. We're saints with the power of the Living God at our core. We have the Life Jacket within us!

Rather than white-knuckling our experiences looking for an escape or a rescue while the water rushes in, we can actually get into the water with our Life Jacket, set our feet upon the Solid Ground beneath us, and *whelm* from what (Who) is inside us rather than be defeated by what's *outside* us.

Remember the Bible story of Jesus calming the storm? (It's in three of the gospels: Matthew 8:23-27, Mark 4:35-41, and Luke 8:22-25.) Luke 8 says the boat was being "swamped" during the storm while Jesus slept on it. (There's no way I would have been able to sleep while my canoe was being swamped! I bet the disciples felt the same way!)

Notice it wasn't the storm that awakened Jesus. It was His disciples. Plus, even though they were all in the boat with Him, we only read three examples of their exclamations.

"Lord, save us! We're going to drown!" Matthew 8:25

"Teacher, don't you care if we drown?" Mark 4:38

"Master, Master, we're going to drown!" Luke 8:24

And here's what I probably would have said: "Jesus, wake up and *do* something!" (I'd be shaking His sleeping body vehemently to make sure He wakes up and fixes this.) "We're all about to die in this horrible storm, and you're sleeping??! C'mon, Mr. God-man, do something *now*!!!" (I'm not proud of how disrespectful I would have been by the way.)

The disciples were clearly overwhelmed. They were feeling hopeless, helpless, and desperate. The Bible records that Jesus commented on the disciples' fear and lack of faith and then simply got up and calmed the storm.

It used to perplex me that Jesus rebuked the disciples as well as the storm. (Of course they were afraid!) However, consider that the disciples were still operating from the outside in. The Presence of the Lord was not yet *within* them, so their security and peace was just as volatile as the storm around them.

In other words, they did not yet have the power of the Holy Spirit residing in their core (not until Acts 2), so even though they were *with* Jesus, they were not yet operating *from* His Presence. Their minds easily went to fear, despair, and doubt rather than faith, peace, and trust.

Live a life *fully whelmed* with the Presence of the Lord and you will not be overwhelmed in the presence of a storm.

SOME "FULLY WHELMED" POSSIBILITIES

How would a disciple who was fully whelmed with Jesus's Presence inside him have handled being in that storm? Here are some possibilities. (Let's call the fully whelmed disciple "D.")

Option 1: They're all on the boat, Jesus falls asleep, and a storm starts brewing. D notices the storm is coming on strong and he also knows the power of Jesus, so he calmly and rationally goes over to Jesus, gently places his hand on Jesus's shoulder to wake Him, and says, "Hey, Lord, would you like us to ride out this storm nestled next to you or would you like to just command it to be still?" (D is surrendered to Jesus either riding it out with them or eliminating the storm completely.)

Option 2: D notices the storm is coming on strong so he goes to the edge of the boat and says, "Storm, the Presence of Jesus Christ, the Word of creation is here, so by His authority, be still!" (D is not trying to control the storm himself. He is ushering in the Presence of the Lord, Who controls all things.)

Option 3: As the storm increases its intensity, D notices the other disciples getting anxious so he says, "Hey, guys, let's gather around Jesus and ride out this storm by singing praise and worship songs that are louder than the storm." (Again, D is fixed on Jesus rather than on the storm itself.)

It's been over 2,000 years since Jesus calmed that storm, and although we believers are equipped with the power of our Creator for faith, peace, and trust to weather our circumstances, we often let our minds wander to fear, despair, and doubt, which do not come from our living inner spirit. We allow ourselves to become overwhelmed by the water rushing into us rather than allowing Living Waters to whelm from within us (John 7:38).

John 14: 16-20 says this (emphasis mine):

*And I will ask the Father, and He will give you another Advocate to help you and be with you forever— the Spirit of truth. The world cannot accept Him, because it neither sees Him nor knows Him. But you know Him, for **He lives with you and will be in you**. I will not leave you as orphans; I will come to you. Before long, the world will not see Me anymore, but you will see Me. Because I live, you also will live. On that day you will realize that **I am in my Father, and you are in me, and I am in you.***

Wow! Jesus abides *with* us and is now *in* us! Jesus is in His Father and we are in Him and He is in us. Let's live *fully whelmed* with Him.

For Reflection and Regeneration

1. Recall (or reread) the canoe-swamping story and what it was like being under the canoe. Have you ever felt an intimate peacefulness like that? Like the rest of the world existed apart from that moment and you felt safe? Describe it in writing.

2. Is any part of a hurricane peaceful? (Look this up if need be.)

   a. What part of a hurricane is peaceful?

   b. When you experience a "hurricane" storm in your life, in which part of the hurricane do you typically reside?

   c. Consider the boat Jesus and the disciples were on during the storm. Where in that boat was the most peace? (Hint: not where the disciples were!)

   d. What part of *you* is the most peaceful? (Think: three circles.)

3. What is a better way to BE other than hopelessly overwhelmed by your circumstances?

4. Spend time in prayer. Ask God to overwhelm you with His Presence. Ask Him to whelm up inside your spirit until you overflow with Him.

JOHN DIAZ DE LION

A Fully Whelmed Cancer Testimony

My wife was pregnant with our second son and our first son was a toddler. Our Pastor was preaching and I had a gut feeling that something bad was going to happen. I never had that feeling before. I was urinating at work and I noticed what I thought was dark colored urine. I called Ruth and she said go to the doctor. I did not.

Three weeks later, early on a Friday afternoon, I noticed it again. I found a coffee cup and filled it with dark tea-colored urine. That was a bit of a shock. I went to the clinic across the street and yes that was blood. The doctor could not find anything wrong, but said clearly urine should be blood-free. That was a long weekend waiting for x-rays and another doctor visit on Monday morning.

I like to talk with people and was having a great conversation with the x-ray tech. When her demeanor changed I knew I was in trouble. Carrying the x-rays to the doctor's office, I gave them to his nurse. I heard them say I had a mass. Well, I've watched enough TV to know what that meant. In a moment I was to find out that at 38 years old I had kidney cancer. It had consumed my entire right kidney. The only solution to kidney cancer, even today, is surgery. If it spreads you're dead because there are no other treatments that really work. Did I cry? You bet. *For the first time in my life, my back was against the wall and I really needed the Lord's help… a miracle.*

But a miracle is instantaneous answered prayer and that's not what the Lord gave me. But boy did He answer prayers. Word went out to many, many friends who prayed for me. Some time after the cancer diagnosis and surgery the following Monday morning, I had God's peace about all this. Passing all understanding, you bet. I didn't know what was going to happen. Every time worry came God's peace was right there. Would I survive the surgery? Would all the cancer be removed? I didn't know, but it was all going to work out, that I knew.

I remember going from the gurney to this real narrow operating table. My legs were hanging over the side with a warm towel on my back and all I felt was peace. I have since described the experience this way: if the Christians fed to the lions in the Roman Coliseum had this peace, the lions were not a problem. My surgeon was walking out of my hospital room before I was going to head home. He turned and said to me that I was the best patient he ever had. Yes, the Lord was there and he answered prayers.

I went through a second kidney cancer just over five years later. I could tell you how the Lord answered prayers this time in different ways, and He was certainly there for me again. I've lived on just a half a kidney for the last 16+ years.

While I call these two kidney cancers my "adventures with the Lord" and I look at them as times He carried me (one set of footsteps in the sand), I'm now on a longer journey. You see, I have cancer again, yes that's three times. It has nothing to do with bad luck because there is no such thing as good or bad luck.

A tiny sliver of blood in a drop of urine on the toilet seat. I always lift it up, but got lazy this one time. Well, bottom line it turned out to be prostate cancer this time. Ruth found the blood. She could have easily missed it. The cancer has already spread to my bladder and area lymph nodes and it's aggressive - a 9 on a 10 point scale. Stage 3 cancer.

You may not understand what I'm going to say next, but I'm thankful to the Lord for the trial I've been through and am going through. He has taken me places in my walk with him that I don't know I could have gotten to otherwise. He loves me more than I'll ever know in this life. I'm looking forward to where I'm headed with Him.

My journey on this Earth still continues. I'm still alive and kicking. I now describe myself as a ship. I have a lot of battle damage, and I am now a bit lower in the water. The reason the ship is lower in the water this time is that other health problems are getting worse. I'm enjoying every drink of water because there will likely be a day when the amount I can drink will be very limited.

Well, most people say to me that I look great. To be honest, it took some time to get the feeling inside that people saw on the outside. It took a while to come to grips that the treatment didn't work. The doctors were honest and said it was likely not to work, but you certainly hope it does.

I'm not in charge of my life. The good things that happen or the bad things that happen. The only thing I can control is my own attitude toward life's circumstances. Is it frustrating continuing to take on water? Yes, of course it is, but what can one do? God's the potter and I'm the clay - meaning He is in control of my life, molding me through circumstances into what He wants for me and what He wants me to be. I know that life is hard for many of us. For me, I know there will likely be many more difficult days ahead.

My engineering career usually was always looking toward the future. Today, I try to take life one day at a time – way different. ...My life's plan is to pray about it and wait on God's answers. I will deal with the physical consequences as they come up (eventually there will be pain somewhere or water retention) or after I see a doctor and medical test results.

I've had over ten doctor visits already this year. I can't remember how many tubes of blood I've donated to the cause. I'm actually doing quite well inside now.

I'm having fun. I've joined the Madison Astronomy Cub, the BMW Club and the Experimental Aircraft Association - EAA. I still attend local IEEE lunches and dinners (an engineering organization). I'm also able to participate in many more church functions that are both educational and fun. I took a trip out east earlier this year visiting museums for ships, planes, cars, motorcycles, and race tracks. There are a lot of long drives between the museums. It gives me time to think, to pray, and to enjoy the scenery of this great country. I spent a lot of time with family. I also spend time with our other kids. Life is going well. I'm finally all in. Want to come?

CHAPTER FOUR

More Than Fight or Flight

My husband gets canker sores. I'm not talking about the little nuisance-type canker sores. I'm talking about the grossly swollen lip, can barely talk, gaping flesh-wound kind of canker sores. He'll pull his lip down for me so I can see the inside of his mouth and I always gasp and wince in sympathy. They look excruciating! We do silly mouth acrobats to aim a gentle little kiss *just right* so as not to disturb the perpetrator of his pain. Or we settle for a peck on the cheek on the opposite side of his face. His canker sores usually appear when he's stressed about something even if he doesn't *feel* stressed. Even if it's a happy occasion. He's tried "all the things" to alleviate it. Sometimes they help a wee bit and sometimes they don't. It's been an on-going issue.

Several years ago I was under a great deal of emotional stress on top of my overfull schedule and responsibilities. I was ready to see a therapist or get counseling or *something* because I was at my wits' end. But I didn't. I was frozen about it all. I did nothing; out of indecision… shame… fear.

Soon I realized how odd it was that I could actually feel my heart beating all the time. It seemed to me like it beat *really* hard. Then I noticed it would skip beats or do two beats at a time and stay like that for several seconds. I'd lay in bed at night and my heart would flip and flop like a fish out of water. It was disconcerting to say the least. I asked Travis to feel my pulse in my wrist. Could he sense the weird heartbeats? Yes, he could. My doctor ordered some testing and based on the results, had me wear a Holter monitor for a couple days. (It's a special vest with electrodes and a recording device to check for heart irregularities.) My diagnosis: "premature atrial contraction."

It sounded like a scary heart condition. The cardiologist said if it changed or worsened to give him a call, but at that time there was nothing he would do about it. Apparently this condition wasn't too earth-shattering.

I told Jesus that I trusted Him with my heart in all ways. I kept giving the premature atrial contractions to Him and while I was at it, He could have everything else in my life too, including my crazy-busy schedule, the millions of unsettling thoughts that kept me awake at night, and the emotionally-charged stress I was experiencing.

I began to spend more time immersing myself in the Holy Spirit and His Word and less time fretting over situations I had no control over. Eventually, the awkward palpitations subsided and my heart beats were not always pounding.

I am convinced that season of heart issues was due to overwhelming stress.

Stress, whether we consider its cause good or bad, shows up in our bodies, thoughts, and emotions even when we don't realize it. Countless studies have been done about our responses to stress. We usually hear fear responses referred to as a "fight or flight response." Our reactions to stress are comparable to our reactions to fear.

MORE THAN FIGHT OR FLIGHT

In recent years, the science community has added more "Fs" to the mix of fight or flight: freeze and faint. Let's look at working definitions of all those.

Fight: fight for survival. A threat means a resistance, implying a battle, whether physical, verbal, or emotional.

Flight: avoid a perceived threat. Run away from it. Escape.

Freeze: unable to act. Go silent. Paralyzed from fear.

Faint: completely shut down. Disassociate. Sleep in response to it.

In addition, Dr Curtis Reisinger, a clinical psychologist at Zucker Hillside Hospital in Queens, New York, told New York Magazine about a couple more adaptations to stress: flood, fawn, and fatigue.

Flood: become flooded with emotions in response to a threat.

Fawn: cooperate or submit to the threat/captor.

Fatigue: (similar to faint) feel tired or sleep in response to a threat.

Okay, we've got some working definitions now. So how do these manifest in real life? What might these actually look like in an overwhelming situation?

I experienced almost all the stress responses (also known as fear responses) within the span of a few minutes. Remember when I mentioned in the first chapter that we'd get up close and personal? Here we go...

A FEARFUL SITUATION

I was a young woman at my boyfriend's house and we decided to go to his basement to watch a movie. Out of nowhere he grabbed my two hands and wrestled me down onto the couch. Caught by

surprise and confusion, I fought back and angrily told him to stop
it (fight response).

But my 125-pound body was no match for his much larger and
stronger body. He pinned me down with all four limbs and brought his
face down onto mine so our eyes were locked, noses nearly touching,
his trembling, raging face seething at me. Suddenly I was frozen. I
couldn't speak or fight back. I felt paralyzed (freeze response).

"How would you like it if I raped you right now?!" He screamed
into my face. "Huh?! I can! I can rape you right now!! Maybe I will!"
He'd lost his temper with me before, but had never threatened me
with bodily harm. I felt hot, terrified tears well up and stream down
my face in fearful disbelief (flood response).

Instantly his face lost its red rage and transformed to mirror my
fear. "Oh, I don't mean it!" he burst out. "I'm sorry I scared you.
You know I would never hurt you." In that moment, I ducked from
under his loosened grip and ran toward the door (flight response).

Seeing my intention, he leaped across the couch, slammed the
door shut before I could get through it, and leaned his back against
it so there was no possible way for me to get through. I knew we were
through forever. I also knew I had to get out of there. "Let me go," I
stated resolutely. "No," he answered back. "I have to leave. Just let me
go!" I pleaded. "No. Because you're going to break up with me and
I can't let you do that. Promise me you won't break up with me and
I'll let you go. You know I'd never hurt you." He was determined.
"Okay, fine. We're not broke up," I replied (fawn response).

Relieved, his face softened and he said, "Can you stay for a little
longer? I mean, let's work this out." I took a deep breath. "Sure," I
said. "Let's just go upstairs together for a little bit." We spent a couple
minutes calmly making small talk and then I said I needed to get
home. He reluctantly released me, satisfied with the outcome of this
episode. And yes, I broke up with him after that, thank you Jesus!

All the previous definitions for the responses to stress and fear are what I'd like to call "Freak Out" responses. (How's that for another "F"?) Am I saying that freaking out in those ways is a bad thing? No. It's not good or bad. It just IS. (In my case, the "flood" response initially broke my captor out of his rage - so it was helpful!) But are the freak out options the *only* ones? I propose another.

THE ULTIMATE "F"

Face it.

Face it: look at stress head-on. Acknowledge the fear around it. Then release the fear (that resides in our soul circle) and choose the courage (that resides in our inner spirit circle).

Gee, that sounds a little too simple, doesn't it? What does that look like?

When my husband gets a canker sore, he acknowledges it, treats it, then moves on with his life. He doesn't complain or dwell on it, he just handles it in stride.

My heart issues began to subside when I was more readily surrendering my literal and figurative heart to Jesus. When I got my wits about me with the ex-boyfriend, I was able to speak calmly and rationally with him until I could get to safety.

The more grounded we are, the more equipped we are to handle the circumstances that could potentially overwhelm us. Because when we're grounded, we're already in a state of "face it."

Fear and overwhelm are closely tied. We're overwhelmed when we're afraid of something. We're afraid of what we can't do, what we'll feel, what we won't have or what we will have. We're afraid of what people will think. We're afraid we'll let someone down. We're afraid of feeling pain, of being left alone, of being ridiculed, of losing someone or something. We're afraid of not having enough time, and consequently of not *being* enough.

So when we recognize that we're feeling overwhelmed, we can ask ourselves, "What *specifically* is overwhelming me about this circumstance?" And then we can ask ourselves what we fear around that. Once we narrow down what we're afraid of in the midst of our overwhelm, we can choose how we want to respond. We can choose to *face it* with courage, peace, and trust because those qualities already exist in us - in our inner core. Thank you, Holy Spirit!

JESUS FACED IT

We will never comprehend the intensity of Jesus's overwhelming burden while He was praying in the Garden of Gethsemane before He was arrested. Luke records it this way in chapter 22: 39-46 (ESV).

*And he came out and went, as was his custom, to the Mount of Olives, and the disciples followed him. And when he came to the place, he said to them, "Pray that you may not enter into temptation." And he withdrew from them about a stone's throw, and knelt down and prayed, saying, "Father, if you are willing, remove this cup from me. Nevertheless, not my will, but yours, be done." And there appeared to him an angel from heaven, strengthening him. And being in agony he prayed more earnestly; and **his sweat became like great drops of blood** falling down to the ground. And when he rose from prayer, he came to the disciples and found them sleeping for sorrow, and he said to them, "Why are you sleeping? Rise and pray that you may not enter into temptation."*

Sweating blood is called "hematohidrosis." It is a rare condition that occurs when someone is under extreme distress. Even *Jesus's* body - in all its humanness - responded to His knowledge of what the immediate future held for Him. The weight of the world was literally upon Him. I wonder, though, if the greater distress and pain was knowing that He'd be separated, even if only for a short time, from the Presence of His Father when He took our place and bore all sin for all people throughout all time on that cross.

If anyone ever had just cause for overwhelm, surely it was Jesus. Yet how did He handle it? He did not fight it, did not run away from it, and did not become paralyzed by it. He didn't allow His emotions to control Him, He didn't sleep it away, and although He cooperated with His captors (to fulfill His purpose in coming to earth), we know His only potential threat was from Satan trying to thwart His glory - and Jesus never succumbed to Satan. He *faced it all* "for the joy that was set before Him" (Hebrews 12:2).

Jesus was never in a state of defeated overwhelm. He was always surrendered to His Father, trusting Him even in the most overwhelming of circumstances. Even when His body was sweating blood while He faced imminent torture and death.

There is no fear in love. But perfect love drives out fear, because fear has to do with punishment. The one who fears is not made perfect in love. 1 John 4:18

Jesus was sinless. All His thoughts, emotions, and actions were pure and holy. It's not that He *wanted* to face what lay ahead for Him (Luke 22:42). It's that He lived as a perfectly righteous human from the inside out. His holy inner core radiated through His soul and every drop of blood-sweat that rolled from His forehead represented His love for the Father and for us.

The result of Jesus facing our punishment meant that *we* would never have to face it. That God would come to earth as a man and die in the most humiliating and excruciating of deaths for our sake is unfathomable.

It's overwhelming.

IN AWE OF HIS GLORY

I was particularly distracted one morning during my quiet time with the Lord. My thoughts were running amuck and I simply could not focus. I prayed, "Lord, what should I do here? I'm having a hard time focusing on you." Immediately I saw myself outside the tomb of Jesus on the third day, just after the stone had been rolled away. I felt confused for a moment. Then I watched as the Messiah Himself emerged from the tomb and stood directly in front of me. He was glowing with an outflow of inner glory and a gentle smile decorated His face. All I could do was drop to the ground in awe and worship.

It was overwhelming.

Ever since then, one of the things I do when I feel distracted or overwhelmed is imagine that scene again. It gets me every time. The love and the power of God far surpass anything my soul is contending with. What else can compare? There is none beside Him.

> *Yours, Lord, is the greatness and the power and the glory and the majesty and the splendor, for everything in heaven and earth is yours. Yours, Lord, is the kingdom; you are exalted as head over* ***all***. 1 Chronicles 29:11 (emphasis mine)

All means all. It means He is even head over the things that overwhelm us.

It means there's no crazy-busy schedule greater than God's love for you or His power within you.

There's no pain deeper than His love for you.

There's no tragedy as dramatic as His victory over death.

There's no betrayal greater than His greatness.

There's no abandonment, rejection, chronic illness, or loneliness that's more overwhelming than the Presence of the Living God.

There's not a numbness stronger than the power of the Holy Spirit.

The same power that resurrected our Lord Jesus from the dead resides within us when we know Christ as our Savior. Are we living from this power or are we letting our circumstances overpower us? Jesus conquered the grave for the former, not the latter.

For Reflection and Regeneration

1. Recall a couple examples from your past when you've experienced any of these F's: fight, flight, freeze, faint, flood, fawn, fatigue.

   a. If you could relive those examples, would you handle them the same way?

   b. What would it look like to "face it" in any of those circumstances?

2. Jesus faced it, all of it, sinlessly. What qualities came from within Him and permeated His soul circle to do that? (Examples might include courage, peace, etc.)

   a. Does that mean Jesus *wanted* every circumstance He encountered? (See Luke 22:42.)

   b. Did that mean He didn't experience emotions? (See John 2:14-16, John 11:35, Matt. 9:36, and Luke 10:21.)

3. To plaster a smile on your face and *fake* "facing it" is exhausting. Facing circumstances that have potential to overwhelm involves whelming up the same qualities Jesus embodied when He lived on earth as a human.

   a. Do you have those same qualities within you?

   b. If not, why? If so, how? (Think: three circles.)

4. Read John 20:10-18. As you do, substitute Mary's name for yours.

   a. Read verse 16 again and substitute Mary's name for yours (again).

   b. Read verse 18 again. How do you think Mary was feeling at that moment?

5. Write three or four things in your life that *could* overwhelm you.

   a. Read and copy John 16:33. *I have told you these things, so that in me you may have peace. In this world you will have trouble. But take heart! I have overcome the world.*

   b. Put a line through the word "overcome" in John 16:33 and replace it with "overwhelmed," which is a synonym for "overcome."

6. Near the three or four things you wrote that could overwhelm you (#5), write what it looks like to *face it* from your spirit, through your soul, and into your body.

ALISHA STAFFORD

A Fully Whelmed Near Divorce Testimony

My husband was arrested for underage solicitation for sex. Praise God, it was a police sting and no minors were involved. But it was a shocking and very public awakening to his hidden sexual addiction. It was all over the news in our medium-size town.

I was so blessed, because the summer before that happened, I experienced a huge personal revival in my faith. I have never felt that close to God or that happy ever! I noticed my husband was a little withdrawn, but I just chalked it up to God and I being so close that nothing else could compare to that. In reality, his sin was a barrier between us, but I was mostly oblivious to his issues.

Fast forward 1 ½ years. We were a month away from finalizing our divorce. I was relieved to be almost free of him and his sin problems, but I was emotional. I walked into my pastor's office and just started sobbing. She said to me, "You don't seem like a woman who is a month away from divorce." "Really?," I asked. "No, usually they are happy." "For real? So, this isn't normal?" "Um, no. I think you need to look at your soon-to-be ex-husband and figure out if something else is going on." "Okay, if you say so....."

It was Wednesday night and we were both at a church function with our kids. During the evening, I looked over at this man who I had been in love with since I was 15 and had had 4 babies (and 2 miscarriages) with, and had traveled all over the country and world with, and I realized that, yup, I still have feelings for him. I ran over to my best friend and I was like, "AHHHH! What am I gonna do??????" And she was like, "AAHHH! I don't know!!!!!"

I went home and started fussing at God. What was the meaning of this? Do You realize how inconvenient this is????? Our divorce is final in a month! I am almost free of him!!! What are You doing????? You told me that divorce was a good option for me!!!! You gave me permission to do that, since he was unfaithful in our marriage!!!!!

The answer didn't come right away. It took a couple days. I was praying and angst-full and for once, thankful that I did not have kids to care for that week because I had some heavy duty praying and waiting to get through.

But finally, God told me what was happening. He said to me, "Yes, I am allowing you to get a divorce. It is a very good and safe option for you. But I have not called you to be safe. I have called you to take risks for My Sake. So, if you are willing, take this risk to care again and see what happens."

There was no guarantee about the outcome.

Two months later, I heard about an organization based in Eden Prairie, MN called Faithful and True. They specialize in counseling people with sexual addiction issues from a Christian perspective. Amazing people! Since most sex addicts are men, they focus on that dynamic. Anyway, they have different weekend conferences, one for the wives, one for the husbands and also couples weekends. Not long after the "I still have feelings for him" epiphany, I found out about this group. There was a wives weekend in a few days, so I signed up. It was wonderful and terrifying and educational, all rolled into one. The best part was we didn't even talk about the men and their issues until more than half way through the weekend! Lol. So, it wasn't just about "Woah is me! My husband cheated on me!" They really built us up as women.

I had always thought there were only two options for you if there was unfaithfulness in marriage: 1. Get a divorce, or 2. Stay married but be bitter about it. But that weekend I learned there is a third option. 3. Both of you get healthy and work hard at healing and you can have an amazing marriage which is a "display of God's Splendor" (that's from Isaiah 61:3, NIV).

But there was still a tiny part of him that was still prideful. His attitude towards me was, "Well, God loves me and forgives me, why can't you?" The thing is, I did forgive him. But that does not automatically mean that he gets to have access to me and my body and my emotions again. He was not a safe person for me emotionally. So, after a lot of prayer and not seeing this bit of pride die, I filed for divorce. And that was the second wake up call for him. Because then he finally realized that he had done everything in his power to destroy our relationship, and my trust, that he ruined our marriage—which freed him to realize that the fact that Jesus loved him was the miracle. I did not owe him anything.

For people struggling with marital unfaithfulness:

Stay in your Bible—even if you don't want to or it doesn't feel like it's doing any good. My old pastor told me that reading your Bible is like medicine. Sometimes you just have to keep taking it in, even though it doesn't seem to be doing anything. You may need to get a bunch of it in you before you see results.

Don't be afraid to tell God everything. You don't need a filter to talk to Him. Have you read the Psalms? David did not have a filter! It is much safer to yell at Jesus about your anger and hurt than to go gossiping around to other people.

But you do need a group of people to pray with you and walk with you through this and to check your thinking with. Just keep it small and confidential! Your pastor is hopefully one of those trustworthy people and isn't scared about dealing with adultery.

Get some professional help. My therapist was amazing! She loves Jesus. I had actually started to see her a year before all this happened because I had anxiety issues. I was just finishing up with her when my husband got arrested. So, we kept on meeting through it all. A week or so after his arrest, she said to me, "Isn't God amazing that we would have this relationship established when your world started falling apart?!?!!?" IS HE EVER!!! So, you never know how He is going to orchestrate your life.

We were able to rebuild our marriage and make it completely different because we were different people after all this. It is amazing. But it has only succeeded because we have both done the really hard work to get healthy. It was not a given that we were going to remarry. When my husband got arrested, it was a wake-up call for him that his hidden sin lifestyle needed to die. He needed to die to it. His relationship with Jesus needed major work, and he was able to come to the place where he fully realized that Jesus loves him!!!

This was the path God used to bring us to wholeness as individuals and ultimately to bring us back together as husband and wife. We don't even count the 22 years of our first marriage. This marriage is an entirely new thing with newly re-created people (which allows for wonderful jokes about our first spouses!!!).

Look to God. He will guide you if you ask Him to and if you are willing to obey.

CHAPTER FIVE

The Hamster Cage

The most fruitful part of my day is my morning devotional time. Jesus and I have spent a lot of time together on my bedroom floor. Sometimes we're hanging out, sometimes I'm pouring my heart out to Him, sometimes I'm listening for His still small voice, sometimes I'm chewing on a portion of Scripture I just read, and sometimes the Holy Spirit puts words or visions into my mind.

Some of us come from a religious background that doesn't believe the Holy Spirit works in this way. So I asked Him if He does or not. (I figured I might as well go right to the Source, since He *is* the third part of the Trinity!) The Holy Spirit answered by giving me more words and visions, which served to deepen my love for Him and others. Plus, when I read the Bible, I see it's loaded with people who received messages, dreams, and visions from the Lord. All this was to bring glory to His Name, draw His people to Him, and to fulfill His plans. He's still into that.

I've experienced more than I could ask or imagine from the Lord ever since I took Him out of my religious box; telling God what He will and won't do with me or anyone else. Now, instead of only knowing all *about* Him, I can also know *Him*. Instead of me doing all the talking and then hoping for the best, we can have a two-way interchange of presence and Presence. I can be with Him while He's with me. His Word is written in His book *and* His Word gets written directly onto my heart. It whelms me from within regardless of my circumstances.

One week, He gave me a vision that came in three parts on three separate days. I recall it almost every day and it reminds me that I can choose *out* of self-induced, exhausting overwhelm when I do *with* the Lord rather than *for* the Lord.

PART ONE OF THE VISION: DO WITH, NOT FOR

Jesus and I were together in a clear glass hamster cage that was lined with sawdust on the bottom and had no top. Inside the cage to our right was a metal hamster wheel. I was so happy to be there with Jesus! *He's always with me, no matter what - even here!*

The cage and its surroundings were well-lit and pleasant. It was clean, orderly, and unoccupied by any actual hamsters (which is good because they'd be huge, considering the cage was proportionate to my size). Smiling in Jesus's direction, I knew what His plans were for me and I was eager to fulfill them. I stepped onto the hamster wheel and focused my attention straight ahead of me, where I could see the goal. My eyes narrowed with intention and I mentally rolled up my sleeves while my legs readied for their task.

True to my nature, I gave it 100%, running in complete focus. The rest of the world seemed almost non-existent while I did my very best for the Lord and for the sake of what He was calling me to do. My head and my eyes remained resolutely focused on the goal and I dare say my form was impeccable on that spinning hamster wheel. I live by "Whatever your hand finds to do, do it with all your might" (Ecclesiastes 9:10) and this was no exception. I was going all out for Jesus.

A couple minutes passed and I began to breathe heavier. In another minute I was winded and my legs were beginning to tire. *Whew! This work for Jesus is tiring, but He's so worth it! I'll give it my best and keep going!* Even though it was tiring work, I was not going to let Him down. I love it when I know exactly what I'm "supposed to" do and can really go for it.

However, by now my energy was depleting, my lungs were burning, and my leg muscles were turning into rubber. Plus, the hamster wheel was spinning so fast that if I were to stop, I'd probably get thrown off. In that brief moment of wondering how I was going to complete this task for Jesus (and wondering what "complete" even looked like here), I glanced in His direction.

He was standing peacefully beside the wheel to my left and instantly I knew He had been there all along. Next I noticed His right arm was outstretched and He was offering me His hand, looking at me invitingly with His eyebrows raised. The hamster wheel came to an abrupt halt (without catapulting me) and then it all made sense.

He wanted me to do this *with* Him rather than *for* Him.

He never asked me to get in the hamster wheel. He probably had His hand ready for mine the whole time and I was too busy focusing all my attention on what I was doing *for* Him.

Dang.

I reached for His hand and stepped off the hamster wheel.

PART TWO OF THE VISION: SUBTLE GUIDANCE

The second part of the vision came the next day. I had just removed myself from the hamster wheel and was holding Jesus's hand. As he guided me toward the center of the hamster cage I realized I could sense where He wanted us to go simply by holding His hand.

It reminded me of when Travis and I hold hands while walking downtown in Chicago or other big cities. When I'm in tune with my hubby and letting him lead our journey, I can feel his hand gently guiding me to stop at an intersection, when to start walking across, when to turn right or left at a corner, and when it's appropriate to speed up or slow down - without a word. More often than not, I'll stand with my toes off the curb while cars whizz past inches away and Travis's hand pulls me back a couple steps closer to the safety of where he's standing.

That's how it is with Jesus. When I'm walking hand in hand with Him spiritually, I can sense His gentle leading. Sometimes I'm like a little kid, digging my heels in while He is moving forward and I'm in a tug-of-war pulling on His arm in disobedience, rebellion, and fear about where we're headed. Other times I'm way out in front of Him, trying to pull Him forward in my impatience, independence, and selfish eagerness.

Jesus is so gracious and patient. The struggle is all mine when I go faster or slower or stand too close to danger. He simply continues to hold my hand without getting off-balance while I'm taken in by my surroundings and wanting to direct the journey.

He doesn't join my struggling and He doesn't let go of my hand.

When I finally focus on Jesus, desiring intimacy with Him and seeking His guidance, I can sense the pulse between our hands and therefore even the smallest shifts in His guidance.

It's as subtle and valuable as the lateral line on a fish. (A fish's lateral line is a system of tactile sense organs in its head and its body that allows it to detect and respond to even the tiniest vibrations and pressure changes in water.) It's the reason fish can swim in schools and also can move quickly toward prey and away from predators.

Oh, to have a lateral line for Jesus - completely aware of His Presence and to move with Him at all times!

Just as all this was dawning on me, a curious thing happened inside that hamster cage. Suddenly, all four of the glass walls burst open at exactly the same time, causing the walls to fall flat from the inside out. Jesus and I were no longer enclosed in a cage, but looking out at the world around us without the confines of the glass walls. Perhaps the glass walls had been a safe haven to protect me from something or someone. Perhaps the walls represented something that had been holding me back or that had kept me in bondage. Whatever the case, those walls collapsed all at once from the inside out. Jesus and I were fully exposed and fully free.

PART THREE OF THE VISION: RISING ABOVE

The third and final installment of this vision was relatively short and occurred a few days later. Jesus and I were standing in the middle of the formerly-walled cage. The hamster wheel was gone so the only thing left of the cage was its floor, which was still covered with sawdust. Ready to be guided by Him, I expected Jesus's hand to lead us forward so we'd no longer be standing on the sawdust. Instead, I felt it begin to move upward with the rest of His body. As my hand clung to His, I began lifting off the ground also! I hadn't even thought of leaving the cage remnants this way, and now we were beginning to rise *above* the entire scene. I knew I was lifting off the ground to fly with Jesus.

That's where the vision ended. Jesus and I were starting to fly together. Once I stopped striving to do things *for* Jesus (which was getting overwhelming and exhausting) and instead surrendered myself *to* Him, I was able to discern His guidance in subtle and beautiful ways. He uncaged me from my own walls. As I leaned in to

Him with trust and unsolicited obedience, I allowed Him to direct me in ways I could not have imagined. My soul became prepared to fly with Him.

What does it look like to "fly" with Jesus? When I completely trust Him, when I'm surrendered to Him, it means I can live a life without limits. I have often put myself in a box by telling myself what I can and can't do and what is and isn't possible in my circumstances. In doing that, I've told God what He can and can't do and what is and isn't possible for *Him*. Isn't that just what the enemy wants? For us to limit ourselves and to limit God? To render God powerless?

I'm taking us both out of my box. Scripture says, "With God, all things are possible" (Matthew 19:26). Who am I to tell myself and God that something is impossible? When I'm overwhelmed, I'm feeling a sense of hopelessness in what I perceive as an impossibility (defeat-based overwhelm). It's the epitome of unbelief. When I choose to believe God that all things are possible, then I will always have hope and will always be willing to step into courage and fly with Jesus. He is all-powerful.

This vision helped me understand that instead of trying really hard to focus on my "work for Jesus," I can entrust myself to Him, surrender to Him and allow Him to take me out of my own caged walls. There's no place I'd rather be than in the gentle yet powerful grip of His hand.

Are you overwhelmed because you're "running the race" in a hamster wheel? Jesus is standing next to you, longing for you to fly *with* Him rather than run *for* Him. Be willing to let Him guide you and expect it to look different than what you've pictured. Surrender control and become so intimate with Jesus that you feel His very pulse - and fly with Him.

The key is "with."

FEELING TRAPPED

Maybe for you, it's not a do-for, performance-driven focus that has you running on the wheel and distracted from Jesus Himself. Maybe it's a situation in which you feel fenced-in and you're hyper-focused on finding a way out. You look longingly at the world around you through those glass walls but you feel trapped by them.

In my vision, my hyper-focus on my goal *for* Jesus distracted me *from* Jesus. Likewise, our hyper-focus on escaping a situation can distract us from walking with Him through it.

Our neighbors across the street, the Bradfords, have owned several dogs. They've had six throughout the past ten years, and all of them have been confined to their yard by an invisible fence (common in our neighborhood). All of their dogs have become notorious for escaping and running rampant. We frequently hear the Bradfords hollering for their pets or see them driving through the neighborhood in search of their runaway canines. Several times I've tried to coax the dogs back into their yard when their owners were oblivious to their escape. In our entire subdivision, the Bradfords' dogs are the only ones I've seen that have gotten loose and run away.

They're also the only dogs in the neighborhood who don't get to go for walks.

When we're not regularly walking with Jesus, we may seize opportunities to run away from circumstances we consider confining. We try to run off on our own because our focus is on our invisible fence (or the glass walls of our hamster cage) and how we can break through and run free. Only Jesus can bring the freedom we're looking for.

FREEDOM IN CHRIST

When we're in step with our Owner, trusting that He's got us no matter what, we are able to walk with Him in the safety and confidence of His care. Our circumstances become opportunities to rely on Him rather than invisible fences that we believe confine us. Our situation might be completely out of our control, but our relationship with Jesus is always within our reach. We just need to take His hand.

Are you hyper-focused on your mission *for* Jesus and neglecting your relationship *with* Him? Or could it be that your desperation to escape your confining circumstance is becoming your primary focus? Look to the One Who wants you to fly with Him in freedom regardless of the circumstances you are in.

The Apostle Paul wrote the book of Ephesians to the saints in Ephesus while he was imprisoned in Rome. Yet, within this "cage," Paul experienced a freedom in Christ that empowered Him to craft Spirit-led letters to the saints. As you read this prayer from Ephesians 3:14-21, substitute the words "you" and "we" (underlined) with your name. May the Holy Spirit speak to you personally through Paul's prayer.

For this reason I kneel before the Father, from whom every family in heaven and on earth derives its name. I pray that out of his glorious riches he may strengthen you with power through his Spirit in your inner being, so that Christ may dwell in your hearts through faith. And I pray that you, being rooted and established in love, may have power, together with all the Lord's holy people, to grasp how wide and long and high and deep is the love of Christ, and to know this love that surpasses knowledge—that you may be filled to the measure of all the fullness of God. Now to him who is able to do immeasurably more than all we ask or imagine, according to his power that is at work within us, to him be glory in the church and in Christ Jesus throughout all generations, forever and ever! Amen.

Let's stay personal with this prayer. Among other things, Paul is praying that we be rooted and established in **love**, that we grasp the **love** of Christ, and that we know this **love** that surpasses knowledge so that we are filled to the measure of all the fullness of God.

So that we are fully whelmed with Him!

Running in a caged hamster wheel vs. flying with Jesus unencumbered is comparable to living from God's whelming love vs. living from fear. When I am focused on what I'm doing for Jesus because that's what I'm "supposed to" do (like in the hamster wheel), I think I'm loving Him. In reality, I'm afraid to disappoint Him. I'm afraid to disappoint others. I'm afraid of failing. It's fear-based.

When we trust Him enough to take His hand, walk with Him, and surrender to His lead, we're coming from a place of love. That's where we can be "filled to the measure of all the fullness of God." That's where we fly (experiencing "immeasurably more than all we can ask or imagine")!

Jesus didn't die on the cross merely because He was "supposed to." He didn't do it out of fear of disappointing the Father based on His performance. He died on the cross because He *loves* us and He *loves* the Father.

But because of his great love for us, God, who is rich in mercy, made us alive with Christ even when we were dead in transgressions—it is by grace you have been saved. Ephesians 2:4-5

...looking to Jesus, the founder and perfecter of our faith, who for the joy that was set before him endured the cross, despising the shame, and is seated at the right hand of the throne of God. Hebrews 12:2 (ESV)

No more hamster cage with glassed-in walls. No more spinning wheel so I can perform for Jesus. No more hyper-focus on *escaping* whatever I think is confining me.

I'm choosing freedom *in* Christ, *with* Christ. How about you?

For Reflection and Regeneration

1. What are some commitments you've made in your life that were *for* the Lord and not necessarily *with* Him?

2. Have you ever dragged behind Jesus, not wanting to go where you knew He was leading? Describe your experience.

3. Have you ever tried to get in front of Jesus rather than wait for His timing? Describe your experience.

4. How do you know when you're walking *with* Jesus?

5. What does it mean for *you* to fly with Jesus?

   a. Can you fly with Jesus in your current circumstances? Why or why not?

   b. Did the Apostle Paul fly with Jesus in his circumstances? Defend your answer.

   c. What is holding you back, if anything, from flying with Jesus?

      i. Where else is this showing up in your life?

      ii. Read Matthew 19:26. What does this mean for you?

6. Have you ever felt confined by invisible fences?

   a. What would freedom look like in that circumstance?

   b. What do you think the Apostle Paul would say if he were in your shoes?

7. In Ephesians, Paul prays that the saints in Ephesus may have power, together with all the Lord's holy people, to do what (verses 18-19)? And for what reason (verse 19)?

8. What does it look like for you to be motivated from a place of love vs. being motivated from a place of fear? Can you give an example?

SONDRA CORBETT-WOOD

A Fully Whelmed Parent Heartache Testimony

I'm currently living in "less than pleasant" conditions with our 17 and 19 year old sons, who have embraced marijuana as part of their daily lives. As a result, our home has been filled with verbal and physical fighting between the two of them at any given time. Their personalities have changed immensely as a result of the high levels of THC they are consuming coupled with the fact that their brains have not fully developed. This causes psychotic episodes, mood swings, and sudden outbursts.

The fact that I'm living in this situation and cannot escape it has caused me to press into a deeper relationship with the Lord than ever in my life (and I'm 56 years old now). Prior to this, I would escape at times by self-medicating with alcohol, which, of course, brought only a deeper level of hopelessness.

There's a scripture that says "My heart is fixed, O God, my heart is fixed. I will sing and give praise" (Psalm 57:7). This is what I decided to do....fix my heart and stand steadfast. Of course, I could not do that without the Lord's help, so I asked Him to give me what I needed to sustain me. He has been faithful on a daily basis.

Equally, the One Year Bible has been a huge answer to prayer in my life, as it has given me a guide for daily reading and providing structure. I look forward to reading each morning as much as I look forward to that first cup of coffee! I believe it took a decision in my heart that I could not do this alone. There was no possible way for me to walk through the intricacies of the events each day held without the supernatural power of God. At each obstacle I faced, I would humble myself, stop, and pray, seeking an answer for what to do in the specific situation.

He has never failed to meet me and help guide me through. Always, His answer was for me to show love. Love had many faces and applications, but it was always a form of His love that He was asking me to give. As I chose this, overwhelming peace would fill and rule my heart.

Since making the choice that I would go nowhere else except to Him for help, God has met me in such an intimate way that my life has been completely changed. What would seem impossible has come to pass. In the midst of severe storms and confrontation, He has Divinely delivered me from deep depression that I was carrying for more than a decade. He has shown me how to live in a place of joy and peace, right while I'm standing in the midst of hostility and unrest. This can ONLY come from God, as it isn't in our human nature.

The main thing I would say to anyone facing difficult situations is that THERE IS HOPE. Nothing is beyond the help of God's strong arm. He sees everything you are walking through and He is more than able to rescue you right where you are. In my case, He didn't have to remove me from my situation (though, if you are in an abusive relationship, that might be what is necessary). He wanted to teach me how to live in Him in the midst of it all. This is what I think overcoming is all about. We are overcomers when we stand in the face of all that is bad, declare His goodness and see Him supernaturally do what no man can do.

I also remember standing in my kitchen one day while fighting was going on all around me. I turned the song "Raise A Hallelujah" (Bethel Music) on as loud as I could and stood in my kitchen, with arms raised, singing that song over my home and family. We can't be passive. We must remember that the battle isn't ours, but God does require us to stand. In standing, we are able to watch Him conquer on our behalf. We don't have to physically escape to be free. Liberty is ours NOW, in the midst of it all, if we reach out and claim all that Jesus paid for and decide that no matter what, we are going to daily live in His presence.

CHAPTER SIX

The Yoke's on You

"Come to me, all you who are weary and burdened, and I will give you rest. Take my yoke upon you and learn from me, for I am gentle and humble in heart, and you will find rest for your souls. For my yoke is easy and my burden is light." Matthew 11:28-30

I s it just me or is the verse about His yoke being easy and His burden light seem like a bunch of malarkey when we're in the midst of overwhelm? There are a whole lot of trials and tribulations in this world that don't seem easy and light! There are so many responsibilities and there is so much busy-ness. When I can barely think because of the flurry of activity around me, that yoke is not feeling easy. When I am so defeated by my difficult situation that I'm not sure how I can survive, that yoke does not feel light.

What does it mean to be in a yoke with Jesus? A few years ago I did a little digging into the concept of "yoke" and "oxen" since oxen are the animals that have most often been yoked throughout history. Among other articles, videos, and online searches, I found a gold mine in Drew Conroy's "Tillers' TechGuide: Advanced Training Techniques for Oxen" as well as the "Living History Farms" website.

As you read the information extrapolated from a plethora of research, notice some hefty parallels, not just in Scripture, but also in our own lives. We'll check out the research first, then discover how it could shed new light on Jesus's invitation to step into His "easy and light" yoke.

OXEN-IN-TRAINING

Before earning the title of ox, a young steer is castrated and undergoes extensive training for about four years. Among other aspects of training, the young cattle learn commands, how to move, and how to be yoked with another steer. (The yoke is a wood structure that is fastened to two animals and connected to a load.)

When young cattle are in training to become oxen, they start with small yokes and as they grow physically and mature in their training, they are given bigger yokes.

But solid food is for the mature, who by constant use have trained themselves to distinguish good from evil. Hebrew 5:14

A team consists of two oxen who share a yoke. The teamster is the master of the team(s) of oxen. (Think of God as our Teamster!) He is their caregiver and leader and works to develop a relationship based on respect, trust, and submission. A good teamster knows his cattle well and calls them each by name.

"He calls his own sheep by name and leads them out." John 10:3b

"Do not fear, for I have redeemed you; I have summoned you by name; you are mine" Isaiah 43:1b

He handles the animals with care, allowing frequent rests and not pushing them too quickly or too hard.

The Lord is my shepherd, I lack nothing. He makes me lie down in green pastures, he leads me beside quiet waters, he refreshes my soul. Psalm 23:1-3

...And his commands are not burdensome, 1 John 5:3b

Cattle that have become oxen at the end of their training have demonstrated to their teamster that he is dominant and in control. If this is the case, it means that the oxen deem him worthy of being followed, respected, and trusted as their leader. They are ever ready to obey group commands as well as individual commands.

You are worthy, our Lord and God, to receive glory and honor and power... Revelations 4:11a

Direct me in the path of your commands, for there I find delight. Psalm 119:35

On the other hand, if the oxen don't follow, respect, and trust their teamster, they will use their own skill or strength outside the parameters of their teamster's training. These cattle are harder to control and tend to challenge the teamster. And if they are allowed to dominate, they are capable of injuring someone out of fear or frustration.

The word of the Lord came to Jonah... "Go to the great city of Nineveh..." But Jonah ran away from the Lord and headed for Tarshish. ...where he found a ship headed for that port. ... and such a violent storm arose that the ship threatened to break up. Then the sailors... asked (Jonah), "What have you done?" (They knew he was running away from the Lord, because he had already told them so.) Jonah 1:1-12

FLIGHT DISTANCE

Like other wild animals, untamed cattle have a natural fear of people. In tame cattle, the distance at which the animal allows a person to approach before it turns to move away is called its "flight distance."

The flight distance of a teamster's steer tells a lot about how it needs to be handled. It's more difficult to train a steer that has a greater flight distance. In other words, it's so afraid of people (including the teamster), that the teamster isn't able to get close enough to train it most effectively.

As a father has compassion on his children, so the LORD has compassion on those who fear him; Psalm 103:13

Come near to God and he will come near to you. James 4:8a

On the other hand, cattle that are used to being touched, herded, and led have a shorter flight distance and consequently are more easily trained. The more they trust their teamster, the more intimate they become, and the more they can rely on the subletest of cues, thereby becoming more productive in their training and in their work together.

So do not fear, for I am with you; do not be dismayed, for I am your God. I will strengthen you and help you; I will uphold you with my righteous right hand. Isaiah 41:10

ATTENTIVE TO THE TEAMSTER

A trained team of oxen has learned verbal cues from their teamster, usually in the form of one or two-syllable utterances. Because cattle have a strong sense of hearing, the teamster doesn't need to yell or even speak loudly to his team. They start by mastering the commands of go ("get up") and stop ("whoa"). When those are mastered, the teamster will teach additional commands throughout the oxen's lives.

"...his sheep follow him because they know his voice." John 10:4

Whether you turn to the right or to the left, your ears will hear a voice behind you, saying, "This is the way; walk in it." Isaiah 30:21

In addition, cattle are very aware of their environment and respond just as well to visual cues as they do to voice commands. The cattle will watch their teamster intently at all levels of training so that by the time they have graduated to official oxen, they can carry out their teamster's wishes without hearing him audibly, using only visual and occasional physical cues.

Since we live by the Spirit, let us keep in step with the Spirit. Galatians 5:25

IMITATING THE SENIOR OX

One successful technique in training cattle is to yoke an untrained animal with a trained ox. Over time the young animal learns what it should do in the yoke by imitating the trained ox.

Follow God's example, therefore, as dearly loved children and walk in the way of love, just as Christ loved us and gave himself up for us as a fragrant offering and sacrifice to God. Ephesians 5:1-2

Regardless of their differing levels of experience, one ox of the two in the yoke will be the dominant one. Let's repeat that statement.

One ox of the two in the yoke will be dominant.

...in all your ways submit to him, and he will make your paths straight. Proverbs 3:6

Once the team has become proficient in the yoke, they can be trained to pull. They will start with light loads and when they've built their strength, endurance and confidence with those, will graduate to heavier loads.

Whoever can be trusted with very little can also be trusted with much... Luke 16:10a

MY YOKE OR JESUS'S YOKE?

Now that we're a little more informed on oxen and yokes, let's check out that passage from Matthew again.

Come to me, all who labor and are heavy laden, and I will give you rest. Take my yoke upon you, and learn from me, for I am gentle and lowly in heart, and you will find rest for your souls. For my yoke is easy, and my burden is light. Matthew 11:28-30

How many times have I taken my own yoke upon myself and told Jesus to come into it? "C'mon Lord, this is going to be great. It's for you anyway. So come and join me. Oh, and bless it too!"

How many times have I felt burdened under my heavy-laden self-made yoke, angry because I felt alone and overworked? How many times have I continued striving in my own strength without even acknowledging the Master? Trying to control my circumstances is exhausting.

Have you ever experienced self-imposed yokes? Like you wanted to make everybody around you happy so you committed to doing this and this and this and this... and you ended up feeling overwhelmed and resentful? And when you told the Lord you needed Him to help ("Jesus, get in my yoke!") you continued to feel resentful because everyone still expected you to follow through on what you committed to? And Jesus didn't solve it for you?

Me too.

We can stop demanding that Jesus join our self-imposed yokes and join His yoke instead.

Being in Jesus's yoke looks more like partnering with the Lord to *love* people the way He does. Loving others does not mean trying to control how they feel (wanting to make them happy no matter what). Instead, it might be praying for them and discerning how God wants to love them *through* you. It's surrendering their happiness, understanding that it's not dependent on you.

We don't need to bear the burden of responsibility for others' happiness. This leads to a defeated overwhelm. When we make ourselves anybody's "savior" or try to be someone's source of joy the situation is hopeless and exhausting.

Because there's only one Savior.

FREEDOM TO CHOOSE HIS YOKE

Sometimes I've taken on too many responsibilities not because I wanted to make everybody happy, but because it seemed like "the right thing to do." Either I was expected to do it, I thought I could do it better, no one else wanted to do it, or I got swept up in the moment and decided to commit. Those were all yokes I placed on myself rather than stepping into Jesus's yoke. My motives in those situations stemmed from a fear of judgment, pride, a martyr complex, or a lack of discernment.

We have the freedom to say no. No to fear of judgment if we don't do what others expect us to do. No to pride because we think we can do it better than someone else. No to being a martyr, and no to getting swept into something without discerning Jesus's heart in it.

When you get asked to do something for so-and-so or to serve in whatever ministry or to join the whatchamacallit group, understand that you do have the freedom to say no.

Because when you have the freedom to say no, you also have the freedom to say yes. Yes to taking time to pray about what's nearest and dearest to the Father's heart. Yes to loving people right where they are rather than trying to be their savior. Yes to letting Jesus be the lead oxen in His yoke, where the "work" of the yoke - God loving people and drawing them to Himself through you - brings peace and hope rather than frustration and overwhelm.

Being in a yoke with Jesus represents not just partnering with Him to love people in His way, but being *connected* to Jesus and to the Father. The beauty of being in Jesus's yoke means that the flight distance between us and the Father diminishes. In fact, it's nonexistent. As Jesus said, "I and the Father are one" (John 10:30).

Further, His yoke *always* stems from a motive of pure love; in seeing what the Father is doing and joining Him in it.

> *Jesus gave them this answer: "Very truly I tell you, the Son can do nothing by himself; he can do only what he sees his Father doing, because whatever the Father does the Son also does."* John 5:19

When we are Christ-like, we do what Jesus is doing because He did what he saw the Father doing. When I am close to Jesus's heart, sharing His yoke with Him, the burden is easy and light because I'm resting in His strength for the heavy lifting. I recognize that I can't bear the burden myself.

> *But he said to me, "My grace is sufficient for you, for my power is made perfect in weakness." Therefore I will boast all the more gladly about my weaknesses, so that Christ's power may rest on me. That is why, for Christ's sake, I delight in weaknesses, in insults, in hardships, in persecutions, in difficulties. For when I am weak, then I am strong.* 2 Corinthians 12:9

When I'm in the yoke with Jesus and I've got no strength, He gets to display His power even more because as the Lead Ox, He's in control while I'm next to Him. I'm completely surrendered. I do not need to exhaust myself fighting Him to be the one in charge and in control of all my circumstances.

We are working *with* Him, not against Him, not in spite of Him, and not just for Him.

Our Master Teamster invented Sabbath rest. When we're linked with Jesus, we'll work with Him from a place of rest, peace, joy, and love, not performance, striving, frustration, or resentment.

I'm going to choose Jesus's "love yoke."

Which yoke will you choose?

For Reflection and Regeneration

1. Reread the information about oxen training. Circle any sections that resemble the Lord and underline any parts that resemble you.

2. What are some qualities of God, our Teamster?

3. How can you relate to the oxen that are being trained?

4. Consider your flight distance with the Master Teamster. What, if anything, would you like to change regarding your flight distance with Him?

    a. Take this a step further and consider your flight distance with two or three people in your life.

    b. What have been some benefits of your flight distance with them?

    c. What have been some costs of your flight distance with them?

5. Where in your life have you asked Jesus to get into *your* yoke instead of joining in His?

6. List examples from your life where you've felt the *burden* of saying yes rather than the freedom of saying no.

    a. What were your motives for saying yes that led to your burden?

    b. What did it cost you?

7. List times in your life where you've felt the *freedom* to say *yes*. What were the results?

8. What are the benefits of being in Jesus's yoke?

SHARON SMITH

A Fully Whelmed Sight-loss Testimony

It was a beautiful spring day on April 18, 2019. My son and I were playing baseball in the backyard, and he had just turned five a few days earlier. We were laughing and having a great time when out of the corner of my eye I saw a white "something" flying through the air. I turned to look and it hit me right in the eye. I blinked quickly a few times and needed a minute to rub out whatever that was that attacked me. Then it was back to baseball.

Over the next few days my right eye would suddenly blink very quickly, as if something was in my eye, like a lash. Some time though, over the week, the corner of my eye got a red line. I thought I broke a blood vessel or something and didn't think much of it. By day five I was experiencing stinging, burning, itching and that feeling that something was in my eye. I finally went to the optometrist eight days after our backyard ball game. I was given an antibiotic/steroid drop, told to wear no contact lenses for a week, and to return for a follow-up.

I needed to stay on the drops for another week. Week three showed the same: a trace amount of irritation and inflammation. I continued with the drops and returned every week for check ups.

At the end of June I saw my first cornea specialist. By early July my vision was changing. My summer was blown. My son's summer was blown. I was rarely ever driving because seeing multiple lanes on a one-lane highway is scary and not safe.

It was now late August. My eye was very red, burning and stinging. My doctor said he thought we better do some scrapings and culture for fungal infections, bacterial infections and acanthamoeba. Acanthamoeba is a very rare eye infection. Amoebas attack and eat the cornea. I endured eleven scrapings, most of which I didn't feel because during this eye trauma of the past four months my nerves were damaged, leaving my eye with little to no feeling. The doctor was almost certain it was acanthamoeba. These amoebas are strong, tough, hard to kill, and made even stronger by four months of misdiagnoses and steroid drops.

As early September rolled on I'd have days where I couldn't see the houses across the street. On other days I could but they looked cloudy. I was losing my sight.

I WAS LOSING MY SIGHT!!!!

The light sensitivity was brutal. I couldn't handle any amount of light. I was in bed for almost six weeks, in the dark, in pain, scared, not momming my son, not wifeing my husband. Isolated. My worst fears of going blind were becoming a reality.

I believed I deserved this. I did some awful things in my 20's and 30's. Certainly not the girl my mom raised me to be. Not the Christian I was raised to be. This was God getting me back for those things. All those mean things I did to others. All those lies I told. So God was saying, "You feared blindness since you were seven years old on the swingset in the backyard staring at the sun. You've done some horrible things in your life to people. Now I'm going to do something horrible to you. I'm taking your sight."

I prayed for forgiveness. I had prayed for forgiveness for years when I did those things I'm not proud of. And sometimes I believed that God forgave me. But I couldn't forgive me. I was in a dark place. I didn't want to live life with the sight of only one eye. I wanted my life back. But this is karma. So, do I sit in my punishment or do I give up? The Enemy was telling me to give up. That God wasn't there for me. The Enemy and I had it all planned out...how to end my misery.

It was sometime mid September when a lady I worked out with stopped over. Why did she want to come here? Then I remembered my pastor had recently told me that God did not leave me and I will see Him in the everyday person. Was this God coming to my house to sit in my dark bedroom?

Yes, it was God! She came, she sat in my bed, and I poured my heart out. I told my story, I cried, I sobbed, I let it all out. She listened. Intently. Compassionately. We prayed, we hugged. She shared some of her own fears and stories. She told me God doesn't make bad things happen to people to get even for past transgressions. She told me God loves me, no matter what. God is weeping with me. He's saddened with me. He's right next to me through these challenging circumstances. I don't remember everything she said that day, but I vividly remember feeling like everything was going to be okay. I felt a shift inside my body. It was God. God came to me in my darkest time and helped me beat the The Enemy.

That day in mid September is the day I gave in, let go, and just let God. I accepted my circumstance. I felt at peace. I knew with Him by my side I could get through this. I started thinking about what I could be grateful for. I could be grateful for the sight out of my left eye. I could still watch my boy grow, I could still play with him, I could still help him learn to read and write. I could be grateful I didn't experience the extreme pain that most do with acanthamoeba. I could be grateful for all the people who showed up for me and my family. There really is good in this world. So many prayers for me. Many brought meals, helped with transportation and just came to sit in the dark bedroom with me. I was seeing that God was everywhere. He was always right there.

It's been five months since my acanthamoeba diagnosis. I'm still taking drops every day. It took some practice and adapting but my life most days is back to normal. I have a new appreciation for the simple, mundane, everyday tasks. I have a new appreciation for my friends and family. I don't take things for granted anymore. That September visit from God changed my perspective. I needed this circumstance to happen. As hard as it was and still is sometimes, I needed something loud and bold to wake me up.

Will I see again? Only God knows. I have a few factors that make me a bit more high risk but a transplant is not off the table yet. I pray every day for mercy and healing. I pray every day to see the world again with both eyes. I'm not giving up or giving in. And The Enemy...he still tries to creep back into my life every now and then telling me to give up and not to live this way. But I always think back to that day in September when God came to see me. And all the other ways God has let me know He's here and He's got this.

CHAPTER SEVEN

Abundant Scarcity

What is the root cause of overwhelm? We like to blame our circumstances. We feel overwhelmed by too much coming at us. The deluge keeps pouring over us and filling us up with more than what we can hold, more than what we can control. For example:

- I am too busy.
- This person is too overbearing.
- I am in too much physical pain.
- This is too difficult for me.
- There is too much injustice here.
- I am too confused.
- I have too many bills/my expenses are too high.
- There is too much clutter in my house.
- I weigh too much.
- I have too many problems.
- I have too many responsibilities.
- My (boss) expects too much of me.

- I am too tired.
- My kids are too unruly/disrespectful/messy.
- My (friend's) emotions are too strong for me to handle.
- This temptation is too great.
- There is too much sadness in my world/ the world.
- This process is going too slowly/too quickly.
- I have too many decisions to make.
- My sorrow is too deep.
- I feel too lonely.
- I am too weak.

There is a dramatic irony with overwhelm. Overwhelm makes us feel as though there is *too much* of something. In reality, we are experiencing a scarcity mindset. Check out the scarcity that is reflected in the following statements. (Note: all the statements reflect a possible negative thought pattern. That doesn't mean they are true!)

- Too busy = not enough relaxation time
- Someone is too overbearing = not assertive enough
- Too much pain = not enough comfort
- Too difficult = not easy enough
- Too much injustice = not enough fairness
- Too much confusion = not enough understanding
- Too many bills = not enough money
- Too much clutter = not enough organization
- Weigh too much = not healthy enough
- Too many problems = not enough solutions
- Too many responsibilities = not enough capacity
- Someone expects too much of me = not able to do enough for them
- Too tired = not enough sleep/rest

- Kids too disrespectful = not enough respect
- Emotions too strong for me = not enough stability
- Temptation too great = not enough self-discipline
- Too much sadness in world = not enough happiness in the world
- Process too slow/too fast = not enough patience/not enough acceptance
- Too many decisions = not enough wisdom
- Sorrow too deep = not enough joy
- Too lonely = not enough companionship
- Too weak = not strong enough

Overwhelm is about scarcity, which happens to be one of the enemy's specialties.

THE ENEMY'S INTENTIONS FOR US VS. JESUS'S INTENTIONS FOR US

The thief comes only to steal and kill and destroy. I came that they may have life and have it abundantly. John 10:10 (ESV)

The thief, good ol' Satan himself, is purposed to steal our peace and joy, to kill our souls, and to destroy our lives. When we allow him to do that, we are living a life of overwhelm. We have an over-abundance of busy-ness, pain, problems, etc. We are living in defeat because we are living in scarcity of the goodness of God. On the other hand, Jesus said He came that we might have an abundant Life; one filled to overflowing with His goodness.

What *is* an abundant life? Does it mean having ten million dollars in the bank? Actually, that's a circumstance - just like it's a circumstance to live in a shack in the middle of nowhere. An exorbitantly wealthy person could still agree with 21 of the 22 items that reveal "too much" of the negative and exist from a soul filled with scarcity. And a materially impoverished shack-dweller could actually be living a more abundant life than the deca-millionaire.

Is God's goodness - His abundance - dependent on our circumstances? If God's abundant goodness is *not* dependent on our circumstances, that means He is inherently abundantly good regardless of how we choose to process our circumstances.

Furthermore, if His Spirit resides in our core, don't we have His abundance residing in us? We can choose to live from that abundant place or from a place where we let our *circumstances* dictate whether we "feel" abundant or scarce.

SCARCITY OR ABUNDANCE OF THE SOUL

Remember the three circles? (Refer to the "I AM in Three Circles" Chapter if you need a refresher.) When we know Christ as our Savior, the center circle, our spirit, is filled with all the beautiful, good, pure, wholesome, joyful, peaceful, abundant qualities of God! It's our soul (our thoughts and emotions) that can operate from a scarcity perspective. As Joshua 24:15 so eloquently puts it: "...choose for yourselves this day whom you will serve..." And as Matthew 6:21 states, "For where your treasure is, there your heart will be also." Is your heart focused on what's lacking in your life (too much of the negative) or is it focused on the goodness and abundance of God?

Satan wants us to feel overwhelmed by our circumstances because that's all he's got to work with to steal, kill, and destroy us. That's what he used in the Garden of Eden too. The circumstance was that God had instructed Adam and Eve not to eat from the tree of the knowledge of good and evil.

The circumstance in and of itself was neutral because facts are neutral until someone places a judgment on them. The enemy took that neutral circumstance and twisted it into something negative in the eyes of Adam and Eve. In their new mindset of scarcity, they were persuaded that eating from all the other trees in the garden was *not enough* (too much restriction) and that they weren't like God *enough* (too human) even though they were made in His image.

Our Creator wants us to be overwhelmed by *Him* - by His unconditional outpouring love, His outlandish grace, His pure goodness, His glorious majesty, and His desire to have a relationship with us. Consider that in the Old Testament, it was actually dangerous to be in His Presence because His glory was so overwhelming that humans would die in His Presence. They couldn't handle His overflowing abundance of glory. In the New Testament, because Jesus redeemed us, we can not only be in the Presence of His Father and ours, we can carry that Presence within us.

Astonishing.

The more overwhelmed I am by Him and His glory, the more His glory whelms within me and flows out of me.

Any circumstance we perceive as negative pales in comparison to the goodness and abundance of God. He is the author of our very being and we get to decide how much of His story He tells through us. Is our story in this life one of being buried by our circumstances or is it one of God's abundant goodness whelming from within us regardless of our circumstances?

There are plenty of people who appear to have it all in this life, yet are miserable. We all know people who can find something to complain about even in the best of circumstances.

Then there are people like Nick Vujicic who was born with no arms or legs and overflows with the joy of the Lord, taking it on the road and speaking to people all over the world about how awesome our God is. Or like Corrie ten Boom, who survived the horrors of a Holocaust concentration camp after she and her family helped smuggle hundreds of Jews to safety. Until her death in 1983, she joyfully traveled and spoke extensively about forgiveness and the love of God.

There are people who are so filled with the Light of Jesus that even though they lost their child, their spouse, or another loved one, in their deep sorrow they will still shine. That Holy Presence is there and overflowing along with the tears.

So how do we get to that place of overflow amidst circumstances that threaten to overwhelm us?

Only through a relationship with the One Who's bigger than our circumstances.

FINDING OVERFLOW IN THE OVERWHELM

I love spending time with Jesus in the morning. Many days, I get on the floor of my bedroom and get into a position of worship like I'm right at His feet. A few years ago I got into the habit of asking Him, "Where are we today, Lord?" and I pictured myself worshipping Him in a different scenario each day as I entered into prayer. I still do that often because it's so fruitful. Sometimes Jesus and I are in a meadow on a sunny day, sometimes we're in the hustle and bustle of the streets of Jerusalem, and occasionally I'm at the foot of His cross. Sometimes we're sitting on the banks of the Jordan River or we're in the Garden of Gethsemane or on the Mount of Olives. We've spent time together in a lot of places!

One morning I was particularly burdened with fear, worry, and anxiety. The icy fingers of overwhelm were threatening and it was difficult to focus my attention on the Lord. I got on my knees, knowing full well there was nothing I could muster in my own strength to eliminate my funk.

This was a job for Jesus.

"Where are we today, Lord?" I asked, as I've done so many times before. Instantly, I saw myself at the tomb of Jesus. The stone had just been rolled away and my anxiety became intertwined with curiosity about the scene I was beholding. Suddenly, there was the risen Lord standing directly in front of me. In that moment all my fear, worry, and anxiety melted away and I became overwhelmed in awe of Who was before me. Neither of us spoke. He was revealing Himself to me as the risen Christ and I was flabbergasted as I beheld His Presence.

There were times when I had been with Him at the foot of the cross and I was aware of His great *love* - that He would go to those lengths to be in relationship with me. Now I was experiencing the first moments of His resurrection, where He could display His great *power* to defeat sin, death and anything else that could come between us. I was overwhelmed by His Presence and nothing else seemed relevant enough to give it my attention. All else became a non-issue and paled in comparison to His greatness.

ENOUGH IS ENOUGH

God (and His grace, power, and love) is enough.

And because He is enough, I am enough.

I have enough.

I can do enough.

There is enough time for what's on His heart.

There are enough resources to carry out His plans.

In fact, God is *more* than enough. He's abundant. And because His Spirit resides in me, so does His abundance. We can live a life that is so filled with awe and gratitude for Who He is, what He's done, and what we have in Him that it overflows from within us.

It whelms us.

COMING TO JESUS FROM MY SCARCITY

Recently I was feeling defeated (again) by all my "not enough" thoughts. (I am a work in progress!) I sat with the Lord in utter distraction during my morning quiet time. I wanted Him to fix my "too much" circumstances and to quiet my mind. To bless me in my chaos. In an attempt to clear my mind and focus on Him, I imagined He and I were sitting together at the ocean, overlooking the pre-dawn beach.

The Holy Spirit took over from there. I looked into Jesus's face and I said, "What do you have for me today, Lord?" (I have never asked that before or since.) I distinctly sensed His immediate response to me. "What do you have for *me* today, Lisa?" My reply, "Well, I have a lot on my plate today. I can't manage it all without you, so I'll dedicate each part of my day to you. I invite you into all of it." Committing to focus on Jesus throughout the day in the midst of all I had going on sounded like a pretty good reply to me. Surely He would give me some encouragement or a special blessing for that.

However, the Holy Spirit didn't grant me a reassuring spiritual hug for my good-girl-at-Sunday School answer. Instead, I felt Jesus lean in towards me and whisper gently, "Watch what I can do." He then turned to face the ocean and look out at the horizon. I started to ask, "What are you...?" and immediately He put his index finger over His mouth to say, "Shhhhh." So I looked out at the ocean too, curious. The sun was just about to peak above the horizon. "Oh! Lord! The sunr..."

Jesus shushed me again.

Without taking his eyes off the imminent sunrise, he motioned for me to be quiet. It finally dawned on me (pun intended) that the One Who created the sun wanted me to sit quietly with Him and watch it rise. I sat and watched for a moment until I felt a praise song whelming and began to sing.

Again, I got shushed.

Jesus shushed me three times! Why did it take three shushes from the Almighty to quiet my soul? I finally got it. He wanted me to clear my mind *completely* by simply observing the sunrise with Him. *His* sunrise. Silently. For as long as it took.

I fully engaged in the beauty of the moment and relaxed next to Him while the sun rose. Have you ever watched the phenomenon? There is a bewildering dichotomy of waiting patiently for the sun to climb inch by inch into the sky and yet afterwards, realizing how fleeting those precious moments were.

There is abundance in every moment if we simply engage in it.

COMING TO JESUS FROM HIS ABUNDANCE

Jesus, the Word of creation (John 1), wanted me to behold the simplicity and the magnitude of the sunrise. He invited me to "Be still, and know that I am God" (Psalm 46:10). I was awestruck by my Lord once again. I could not recall anything that was plaguing my mind prior to watching the sunrise with Jesus. I had lost myself in His magnificence and in the invitation to observe His glory through His creation.

Then I recalled the question I had posed earlier, "What do you have for me today, Lord?" and His reply, "What do you have for *me* today, Lisa?" My response to Him came quickly and from deep inside.

"Jesus, you have my heart," I said, facing the One Whose abundant love, provision, and power owns my heart just as much as He owns the sun in the sky.

"You have mine too," He said.

And that was enough - more than enough - for both of us.

Because of that experience with Him, I now process my overwhelm differently. I thank Him for Who He is, what He's done and will do, and what I have in Him. He paid for my heart, so He already has that, and I know I have His too. What else could we have for each other that's greater than that?

And with that perspective I can do a little self-coaching when I begin to feel overwhelmed. Maybe this could help you too.

1. Ask yourself what *exactly* is overwhelming you. (What specifically feels like "too much?")

2. Look at the flip side and ask yourself what you think is *lacking* in your situation?

3. Worship the One Who created the world and you and everyone else. Focus on His greatness.

4. Tell Him (and yourself) that because He's not lacking, neither are you. He *is* more than enough. He's done more than enough, and He's given more than enough.

Here's what that could look like:

Lord I feel overwhelmed right now. I have too many deadlines, demands, and responsibilities. I have too much on my plate - things that will affect sooooo many people. I feel pressure. I feel anxious. I don't have enough time. I'm spread too thin. There's not enough of me to go around. So many people will be disappointed by my lack here! I am not enough for all this!

Lord, you created time. You're beyond time. You are the Alpha and Omega. You're the King of Kings and the Lord of Lords and You alone are worthy of all praise and honor and glory. You're greater than the universe and yet You know how many grains of sand are on the beach. You created me. You know how you can and will use me. Help me to trust in You alone and not in my performance. Thank you for all the blessings you've poured out and continue to pour out. Thank you for the beauty of your creation, for what you did on the cross and in the tomb, and for the peace and strength I can have in you. Lord, I am nothing without You and You are everything to me. You are in me. You are more than enough for me. Pluck out of me what isn't Yours and help me to receive Your love and give Your love in the things I am doing now. Because that's enough. Amen.

I wrote one of my favorite verses on an index card and keep it handy for when I begin to feel overwhelmed and "not enough."

And God is able to bless you abundantly, so that in all things at all times, having all that you need, you will abound in every good work.
2 Corinthians 9:8

For Reflection and Regeneration

1. List some things in your life that could be overwhelming to you.

    a. Identify what is "too much" in each of those.

    b. On the flip side, identify what is "not enough" in each of those.

    c. What does the enemy want you to believe about those circumstances?

    d. What does Jesus want you to know about those circumstances?

2. Vocabulary.com describes the word "revel" with the following: "Revel means to take great pleasure. If you revel in something, you're not just pleased or even excited; you're overwhelmed by joy."

    a. In what aspects of the Lord's creation do you revel?

    b. If God is all-powerful, can He hold you through your overwhelming circumstances?

    c. If you trust that He can hold you through those circumstances, you can choose to focus on taking great pleasure in Him and in His creation. Find a few Bible verses that remind us to find joy and/or contentment in any circumstance and write them out. (Hint: check out James 1, Philippians 4, and 1 Thessalonians 5 among others.)

JOEL BARAKA

A Fully Whelmed Third World Testimony

I was born in the Democratic Republic of Congo. However, a few months later, civil war broke out in my home area and my family was forced to move and seek refuge. We moved to Uganda in East Africa and ended up in Kyangwali Refugee Camp in western Uganda.

Growing up in Kyangwali, I would see my parents work in the fields from sunrise to sunset to provide for the family. When I started school, I overheard my teachers talk about how with education, every child had a chance to live a better life. With this, I thought it was the right time to take school seriously. I promised myself that I would show up every day and do my best for better results in school with the hope that this would open up doors for me.

Because I grew up in a Christian home, I have always known what it meant to be a Christian. From an early age, I knew that God in Heaven was a caring Father, and that prayer was one of the ways to communicate with Him. My prayer was the same every day. I asked God for blessings with knowledge and strength to do well in school so I could one day finish school and get a job that would give me monthly pay to support my family.

Luckily, in 2015 I landed an opportunity to study in South Africa at African Leadership Academy, my dream high school and one of the continent's finest. It was an exciting time and probably one of the most life-changing times for me. God had answered my prayers and life made a lot of sense until my senior year approached and the question of what college I should attend was becoming a big deal.

Soon, college essays were piling up and things didn't seem to go my way any more. I started feeling overwhelmed and as if I were drowning. This left me wondering whether there was something I wasn't doing right and that maybe God was disappointed with me. I never doubted his existence, but I questioned whether He had forgotten me. I was still doing my best and every day I showed up with the same commitment and the same strong desire of helping my family one day.

Soon I felt I couldn't deal with this any more and thought I probably needed to talk to someone. I reached out to one of my chaperoning pastors and openly shared what I was going through. In the middle of the conversation he looked at me in the eyes and said, "Joel, if you can focus more on giving thanks, then you will have a great time, not just here at the academy but throughout your life." We both paused for the next few seconds. His few words set a new tone for the rest of my high school journey and undoubtedly the rest of my life. I remember thinking to myself, "Man, all this time you have just been asking and just taking from God and never deeply saying thank you to God for all He has done for you!"

At that point, I walked into my room and decided to write down all the things I was grateful for: having a caring family, food to eat, friends who cared about me, clothes... The list was endless! I began crying like a little child. It was beautiful though. They were tears of joy, for I had learned my lesson.

Since then, I decided to be grateful for how far God has brought me and the countless opportunities he has placed at my feet. This has not only brought me peace but has truly excited me about His plans and the purpose He has placed on my life.

My university application process went so fast. I was accepted in two universities, both on full scholarship, and the University of Wisconsin Madison happened to be one of them. Now here I am in my third year doing my B.S. in Civil Engineering.

For sure, once in awhile I get nervous about the future. But every time I look back at the countless scenarios and I see how God has shown up for me, I am more encouraged. I still want to show up every day and do my best in whatever I do, but most importantly, I hope not to let circumstances lead me into questioning God's presence in my battles. He has been there for me in every situation. He is worth trusting, for I know that He did not bring me this far to leave me.

CHAPTER EIGHT

Chocolate and M & Ms

Let's take our relationship to a new level: chocolate. Yes, I'm calling "chocolate" a level in a relationship. Something happened to me when I entered my 40's. What I formerly considered merely a vehicle to get caramel into my mouth became a craving in and of itself. Caramel took a back burner to my new-found fetish: dark chocolate. It is delightfully sweet, deep, rich, authentic, smooth, slightly caffeinated, and though it's quite satisfying, it always leaves me wanting more later. Sounds like a great friendship.

My mother-in-law is also a chocolate lover. When we gave her a couple sample chocolate bars from cocoa beans native to the places we had just visited, she said, "I'm going to eat these later when I'm by myself so I can take my time and savor each bite." She texted a couple days later and said she ate them both in one sitting. I pictured her setting aside time in her day, fully engaging in each bite of that cherished chocolate until it was gone. It was a blessing to know she valued the gift as much as I did.

I consume dark chocolate nearly every day. I also take supplements every day. What a difference in how I approach ingesting both of those! I take my supplements with maximum efficiency, putting a wad of capsules and tablets into my palm and gulping them down with one huge swallow of water. I take two fistfuls of supplements and immediately move on to my next task for the morning, checking "supplements" off my mental to-do list. My motive for taking them is different than my motive for eating dark chocolate. The supplements help my body systems to be at their best (even though I don't understand the exact science behind them all). I take them because they're apparently good for me. The dark chocolate, however, is for pure enjoyment. (Dark chocolate happens to have some great health benefits too - yay!)

Is your relationship with your Creator like taking supplements more than it's like enjoying dark chocolate? Maybe you read the Word, swallowing a bunch of verses each day because you know at some level it's good for you even if you don't exactly understand what you're reading. Maybe you spend some time in a devotional book every day, say a few prayers, and then cross that part of your day off your to-do list.

Or perhaps time with the Lord is too inconvenient so you tend to avoid it until you have more motivation (like a "serious" prayer request that's actually worth talking to Him about).

Our God wants us to enjoy time with Him like my mother-in-law and I enjoy dark chocolate. That time with Him is also precious because it enables all our systems within our three circles to be at their best, being fully influenced by His Presence. The Holy Spirit wants us to savor being with Him like He savors being with us. If God didn't want to be with us, He wouldn't have gone to such great lengths to ensure that we could spend eternity with Him - starting with our time here on earth.

SAVOR CONSISTENTLY AND AVOID
SUPPLEMENTAL CRAMMING

Have you ever experienced a lecture, sermon, or presentation where your eyes begin to glaze over and your mind wanders? Me too. I had a professor in college named Dr. Ohl, who was a great teacher with a great passion for his field - plant biology. However, my level of academic engagement in the lecture hall was lackluster at best. The silver-haired botany phenom obviously loved what he did, but I didn't share his affinity for botany. So rather than studying his words and diagrams, my focus was on his eyebrows.

Yes, his eyebrows.

Dr. Ohl's thick gray eyebrows stretched so far beyond his glasses they seemed to be reaching toward me regardless of where I sat in the lecture hall. How could I take notes on endoplasmic reticulum with eyebrows like that perched just a few inches above my professor's mouth? His lectures were the "necessary supplements" my brain needed. They were apparently good for me. But those eyebrows captured my attention and I chose to be distracted by them.

When midterms approached I panicked. A large percentage of our grade was going to be based on the lectures and I didn't know the material. The information I could have savored when Dr. Ohl had presented it now became a supplemental cram session with a textbook in an effort to pass the test.

If our relationship with the Lord is primarily a "cram session" when the going gets tough, overwhelm is sure to set in. Being overly-focused on the minutiae of our circumstances leaves us empty of the rich depth of the peace of Christ when we face substantial trials. On the other hand, when we've been consistently engaging with Him and savoring the wealth of His Presence daily, we are far less vulnerable to defeated overwhelm. We don't need to cram Jesus into our trials because we're accustomed to being with Him and surrendering everything to Him already.

Turns out I missed the big test because I got pneumonia and ended up in the hospital for the entire week of midterms. I re-enrolled in the course the following semester (with Dr. Ohl again!) and kept meticulous notes for every lecture. I treated the lectures like dark chocolate, hanging on every word and fully engaging with the material. Midterms and finals were not nearly as threatening and I closed out my semester with an A-. Lesson learned. When I engage with the professor and embrace all he has for me, I don't go into panic mode for the tests.

When I'm consistently engaging with my Creator, I don't go into panic mode when the going gets tough.

IDENTIFYING WITH M & MS

Time to break out the M & Ms: Mary and Martha. Most of us have heard their story so many times we skim over it or tune out. There have been countless books, studies, videos, etc. about Mary and Martha. I used to roll my eyes when someone would bring these two ladies into a sermon or a book because I identify so closely with Martha (the busy one) that all I could feel was guilty that I wasn't more like Mary (the one who sat at Jesus's feet). It was like extremely bitter chocolate. Great idea 'cuz it's in the Bible and all, but I didn't know how to process my being the "bad one" of the two sisters. (After all, *somebody's* got to get stuff done!)

Turns out Martha's not "the bad one." In fact, Mary and Martha were a lot alike. For one, Jesus had a relationship with them and loved them both.

Now Jesus loved Martha and her sister and Lazarus. (John 11:5)

Another fascinating similarity is that they both used the same words with Jesus while He was on His way to Bethany to raise Lazarus from the dead. Martha, when she heard He was coming, ran out to meet Him and said, "Lord, if you had been here, my brother would not have died" (John 11:21). Likewise, Mary, who had stayed back in the house until she was called by Jesus, also said to Him, "Lord, if you had been here, my brother would not have died" (John 11:32).

Both sisters were grief-stricken, both called Jesus "Lord," and both acknowledged their faith in His ability to have changed the outcome for their brother.

Notice their differences here, though. As soon as Jesus was approaching Bethany, Martha ran to Him and spoke the words about her brother not dying had He been there. She followed them with, "But I know that even now God will give you whatever you ask" (John 11:22). She appealed to His authority to rectify the circumstance. It was almost like she was telling Him what to do.

She's pretty assertive, that Martha.

When Martha went back and told Mary that Jesus had asked for her, Mary ran out to Him and "fell at His feet" (verse 32) before she said a word to Him.

Mary *worshipped* Him first.

Jesus's responses to both women was different too. After Martha "reminded" Jesus that God the Father would give Him whatever He asked, Jesus replied with an "I AM" statement and elicited a confession from her.

Jesus said to her, "I am the resurrection and the life. The one who believes in me will live, even though they die; and whoever lives by believing in me will never die. Do you believe this?" John 11:25-26

She needed to be reminded of Who Jesus *is* and be given an opportunity to acknowlegde Him as the Messiah. To savor her Savior.

Mary's heart was already in a place of worship and submission before she told Jesus she believed His Presence would have changed the outcome for Lazarus. Therefore, Jesus and Mary were already in an intimate place of *connection*.

When Jesus saw her weeping, and the Jews who had come along with her also weeping, he was deeply moved in spirit and troubled. "Where have you laid him?'" he asked... Jesus wept. John 11:32-35

Jesus was hurting *with* Mary.

Sometimes in our overwhelm we feel like the Lord is observing our trial at a distance. Perhaps we believe He has a "take your supplements" perspective toward *us*. Like He simply puts up with us because He's *supposed* to. Mary's approach showed that she and Jesus had a two-way dark chocolate kind of relationship. That savored, connected relationship is what He longs for with all of us.

Come near to God and he will come near to you. James 4:8a

Martha was talking *at* Jesus. Mary was connecting *with* Him.

Recall the famous (infamous?) Luke passage where we're first introduced to Mary and Martha.

As Jesus and his disciples were on their way, he came to a village where a woman named Martha opened her home to him. She had a sister called Mary, who sat at the Lord's feet listening to what he said. But Martha was distracted by all the preparations that had to be made... Luke 10:38-40a

Martha invited Jesus into her home and then got distracted by what she was doing for Him. In the meantime, Mary "sat at the Lord's feet listening to what he said."

Mary was *with* Him.

Notice how Martha approached her guest, Jesus.

"Lord, don't you care that my sister has left me to do the work by myself? Tell her to help me!" Luke 10:40

Martha, in her overwhelm, appeals to Jesus's authority by demanding He tell Mary to help her. Oh, that assertive Martha. Jesus's response is spot-on (of course).

"'Martha, Martha,' the Lord answered, "you are worried and upset about many things, but few things are needed—or indeed only one. Mary has chosen what is better, and it will not be taken away from her." Luke 10:42-42

If Jesus spoke to me like that He might say, "Lisa, Lisa, you are distracted and upset by silly things like your professor's eyebrows and drivers who leave their blinkers on. You are worried and upset about things that don't define you, like what people think about you or whether you've crossed off everything on your "to-do" list for the day. Just be with me - choose me *first* - and all those things will be put into their proper perspective. I don't want to be the supplements you *have* to take to be healthy spiritually. I want to be in relationship with you because I cherish you and want you to cherish me too, even more than dark chocolate."

CHECKING MARTHA'S MOTIVES - AND OURS

Martha opened her home to Jesus for what reason? It could have been to bless Him or it could have been for another reason. Luke doesn't record how it came about. Either the Holy Spirit led her to invite Jesus into her home or she invited him for her own reasons. Was she stepping into His yoke or did she create her own yoke? Regardless, when she approached Him, she told Him what to do about her yoke (which obviously was not feeling easy or light to her). She was trying to be the "lead oxen" in that circumstance while simultaneously playing the victim. She was saying, "My sister did this to me and now I'm the only one doing all this work."

We can *be with* Jesus so we can *do with* Jesus. I wonder what would have happened that day if Martha had worshipped Jesus as her Lord and Savior before she got concerned about what she should be doing *for* Him.

I wonder if Martha had treated her service to Him as an act of worship, expressing gratitude to Him for being present with her and savoring every moment of Him being in her house, would she have acted differently? Would she have still felt like a victim to her circumstances?

I bet not.

Martha was not the "bad" sister. At her core she loved Jesus and believed He is the Messiah, her Lord and Savior. Martha simply learned that Jesus wanted *her* more than He wanted her agenda - even when the agenda involved Him.

When our agendas (how we think things are supposed to look) are more consuming than our Savior's presence, we become overwhelmed and are concerned more about the task than about His presence *with* us in the task.

Kind of like my attitude about savoring chocolate vs. chugging my supplements so I can move on to the next thing. Or like running in a hamster wheel for Him until I'm worn out. Or like telling Jesus to get into my yoke instead of meeting Him in His.

I want a dark-chocolate-supplement kind of relationship with Jesus. It's a beautiful, Life-giving relationship to savor, and ingesting His Presence is the best way I can care for this temple of the Holy Spirit (1 Corinthians 6:19). I don't want to be distracted by the "to-do's." I want anything I do to be an act of worship that flows from my relationship with Him.

I want to be like Mary and Martha. Both of them. ("Mare-tha" has a nice ring to it.) Now I like to think of the sisters like dark chocolate

M & Ms in a great big bowl. Some "M"s in the bowl represent Mary and some represent Martha - and they're all dark chocolate. Each day I get a mix of both "M"s. I start my day by savoring the Savior. I align my heart with His and acknowledge that whatever is set before me for that day is His yoke.

He already knows what I'll be encountering each day and He's in it all. I do have goals for my day, and as I mentally and spiritually hold His hand, I step into those goals with Him. This allows me to more readily switch gears or directions as He leads. I used to create a weekly to-do list, which I now label my "opportunity" list. These aren't merely tasks for me to cross off my list. These are opportunities to work alongside Jesus in the day-to-day. Worship and then do. Be with Him first, do with Him second.

I also get to choose to be *with* Jesus in the extraordinarily challenging seasons. I'm already surrendered to Him, so overwhelm is not defeated and hopeless. I don't need to look at a trial as a cram session for prayer just to get through the season. Instead, it's an opportunity to lean on Him and mature into greater dependence on Him.

INTENTIONAL MARE-THA MOMENTS

I got to be "Mare-tha" for an overwhelming circumstance several years ago. About a week before Travis's 40th birthday, he took our teenage son and his buddy to a mountain biking park across town. On their last run through a series of jumps, my beloved husband miscalculated a jump and ended up falling from a height of eight feet, landing on his back.

Because he was in a great deal of pain, we immediately headed to the urgent care clinic where I got to practice my Martha skills with the doctor, insisting that he order x-rays. While we sat alone in the doctor's office awaiting the results, Travis fainted. I simultaneously attempted to coax him back to consciousness while strategically opening the door wider to call for help. What ensued resembled a dramatic medical TV show. Several staff rushed in, put him on a gurney, and instructed me to meet him at the hospital emergency room.

I prayed my way to the hospital between making phone calls to family members. While talking to his parents, I pulled over to let a siren-sounding, lights-flashing ambulance pass. It was the ambulance that was transporting my husband. That moment is forever etched into my brain and heart.

After a series of tests in the ER, we learned he had some cracked ribs as well as an injury on his spine. He would spend a few days in the hospital and get fitted for a body brace, which he would wear for about three months. All we could do was hope for the best in terms of recovery and long-term impact. On his 40th birthday he enjoyed some green jello, thankful to be home regardless of what he was and wasn't able to eat yet.

Travis spent the next several weeks lying flat on our bed, secure in his turtle shell while we (and many other friends and family members) prayed for healing. A couple times a day, we strapped a large belt around him so I could hold onto the loose end and keep him steady while he practiced walking around the inside of the house. We worked through logistics on how to unstrap his shell and roll him in and out of the front and back of it so he could stand in the shower for five minutes every two to three days without wearing it. We developed a routine for how to care for him so he could eat and maintain proper hygiene, and we wondered what life was going to look like in the future for this man who previously, in the scope of just one day, could run a 5k, mountain bike, push-mow our large lawn, and make progress on several projects with energy to spare.

I continued to homeschool our three kids, teach and grade three essay-writing classes, serve at church, coordinate and host multiple holiday gatherings, lead a mom's group, manage the household laundry, prepare meals, clean the house, host visitors, *and* provide primary care for my husband. It was a lot to handle.

Oh, how I needed to be with Jesus in that season! When overwhelm started to creep in, it was because I adopted a Martha-the-martyr attitude in my "do-for" disposition. When I adopted the Mary-the-worshipper disposition, I was not overwhelmed. By starting each day at Jesus's feet and being with Him each morning, I could hold my Savior's hand while we walked together in each part of my day. I savored the chocolatey richness of being in His Presence so that my own presence could reflect His, even in the most mundane tasks. Even when we didn't know how long life would look like this or what the future would hold. Spending time with Jesus each day enabled me to take my supplements (do what I needed to do) knowing that I could find joy in the journey through God's tender mercies. In fact, because He was with me, those supplements started to adopt a chocolate flavor - hence the joy in the journey!

Give thanks in all circumstances; for this is the will of God in Christ Jesus for you. 1 Thessalonians 5:18

Being grateful was like indulging in dark chocolate too. All those things on my plate became opportunities to express gratitude and savor God's mercies in each moment. I became thankful for every small victory, every task completed, every gesture of support from our loved ones, every challenge that I knew God could handle, every day that showed any sign of progress. Every. Little. Thing.

After a while, the little things I was grateful for became bigger things to be grateful for.

Travis had a follow-up appointment three months after the accident. At this point, he was only wearing the turtle shell for part of each day and could practice walking around the house without wearing it at all.

We sat at the doctor's desk, waiting to hear the news about his injuries. We had already seen progress in healing, so we were hoping for the best and we were ready to hear what the long-term effects would be.

The doctor informed us that according to all the x-rays and scans, it looked like nothing had even happened. Nothing. God of miracles! To this day, Travis has never experienced fallout from cracked ribs and an injured spine. When I think about it, I want to fall on my knees in gratitude and worship.

When I recall that season I smile about having a "Mare-tha" disposition. And I can once again acknowledge the immense worthiness of our God for all my praise and then fully engage in whatever lies before me each day.

We have a "dark chocolate," "M & Ms" kind of God. He wants to connect with us in relationship. He wants us to savor being with Him. He wants us to acknowledge how great He is and worship Him. When we're consistently whelmed with Him, we can approach our circumstances - even the overwhelming ones - with ever-present, overflowing peace and gratitude.

For Reflection and Regeneration

1. Do you identify more with Mary (relationship-focused) or Martha (task-focused)?

2. How can you be a combination of both Mary *and* Martha ("Mare-tha")?

3. Is your relationship with Jesus more like taking supplements or more like savoring dark chocolate (or another favorite treat you enjoy)?

4. What distracts you from having quality time with the Lord on a daily basis?

5. What are the things you love about Jesus? Write them down.

   a. After you've written them, label them with "do" (what He's done) or "be" (qualities He IS).

   b. Notice from your labels if you love Him because of what He does AND because of Who He is.

   c. Here's a great distinction between praise and worship: praise is acknowledging what God has done and worship is acknowledging Who He is. Label the list items you just created as either "praise" or "worship."

6. Consider a situation you're in that feels overwhelming. Write 10 little things (or big things) you're thankful for regarding that situation.

ANNE HOGAN

A Fully Whelmed Mom–of–Twelve Testimony

When I had my fifth baby in five and a half years, my brother asked me if I felt overwhelmed. I said "yes" and tears sprang to my eyes.

Later, I analyzed the situation with God and then my husband. Though in the natural, it was a bit overwhelming to think about having five little ones, my husband and I actually had a vision to have a big family, disciple them in the ways of God, and train others to do the same...all to the glory of God! God had been faithful in giving us four children; we knew He would also give us all we needed — spiritually, mentally, emotionally, and physically — with five. I went forward with peace, joy, and hope in God.

How to walk out that vision and access our provision was my question to the Lord. One afternoon I got on my knees and cried out to the Lord, "Jesus, I don't just want to survive; how can I thrive?!!"

I opened my Bible and read Colossians 1:27. The last part stuck out to me as an answer to my question: "Christ in us the hope of glory." Hallelujah! That was it! My God was faithful! He had made provision *for me, His daughter, and our family through me and my husband as we yielded daily, hourly, even moment by moment to His Spirit, Christ, which means the Anointed One, living in us. He was our hope of thriving — thus being able to glorify Him!*

We were not left to our own physical or soul capacities; we had the capacity of Heaven: the Holy Spirit inside of us living and moving through us; the Holy Spirit giving us vision day by day and moment by moment as our hearts were turned to Him and open to receiving from Him. The Holy Spirit led me to access my provisions through humility, discipline, thankfulness, singing, and outside help.

Before my third baby was born, the Holy Spirit gave me revelation of rising up at 5am in order to have time with Him in His Word, prayer, and journaling. Before the children got up, I could also take a prayer walk or jog, start a load of laundry, and prepare a simple but nutritious breakfast for everyone. Then my time with my children began. Granted, when afternoon nap time came, I was the first one asleep!

I experienced being the head and not the tail primarily: being ahead of the game, not behind. It took grace, discipline, determination, accountability, and prayer from others, but it worked!!! Ten years of that schedule while my children were young got us through with flying colors! I still had my challenges, but my family was a beautiful miracle.

A beloved pastor told me in college, "Depression and thankfulness cannot coexist." I needed to learn to apply this because depression from anxiety and being overwhelmed knocked at the door of my heart (soul) more than once! I would say, and continue to say, "Thank You, Lord, for Your goodness. Thank You, Lord, for my wonderful husband! Thank You Lord for each child! (Now I have twelve children, one son-in-law, and a grandson!) Thank You, Lord, for this day, Your provision, protection, angels, and Holy Spirit to fill each of us up to overflowing today and every day! May each of us be taught by You, and may the peace in our household be great! We dedicate and consecrate ourselves to You. Bless us and keep us and use us for Your glory, God." I pray something like this daily at our family devotion time before schooling, and bits of it over and over throughout the day.

I also thank Him for working out everything for the good and for our maturity in Christ. Trials and hardships teach us and cause us to cling to God and desire to walk in His Spirit and His ways. To consistently ward off being overwhelmed and falling into the "pit of depression," develop a lifestyle that involves frequently thanking God (and others) for everything going on in your life...and every provision that is available to you through the Holy Spirit's grace, wisdom, and the help of others.

Colossians 3:16 says that we are to "let the Word of God dwell in us richly, SINGING to ourselves in psalms and hymns and spiritual songs; singing and making melody in our hearts to the Lord." In order to memorize and meditate on Scripture and teach it to my children, I would put Scripture to melody and also sing hymns and other songs that keep me and my family encouraged. When my children were fighting, instead of yelling "stop," I would sing sweetly, "and be kind one to another, tenderhearted, forgiving one another even as God in Christ forgave you" (Ephesians 4:32). It was and is a way to keep calm, flowing in the Holy Spirit, and to give grace to the hearers (my children). It convicts them and gives them direction and vision as to where they need to shift in their attitudes and actions without me giving them a "lecture" or correction.

Have you ever experienced clutter in your home causing stress and the feeling of being overwhelmed? Some research (not sure from where) said it was one of the top reasons for moms being stressed. I believe it! Because we had a vision for having a big family, we knew that we needed to keep our home girded up with order and cleanliness in order for us to have a home of peace and joy. God's character of orderliness is described in 1 Corinthians 14:33 & 40: "for God is not the author of confusion, but of peace; let ALL THINGS be done in decency and ORDER". We have continued to evaluate and create systems in our home that create order in the areas of taking care of our food, shelter, and laundry. One family suggested having the goal of keeping our homes "hospitality ready." Our goal is to keep it clean and orderly enough to be able to have it "hospitality ready" at a half hour's notice. Well, in order for this to happen, especially when my children were young and many, I needed help!

During that season of my life, I would ask God to clarify to me what help I needed, and asked Him to provide help for that specifically. I got help with our home from a teenager that I got to train and mentor in childcare and house cleaning. She helped me clean for two hours weekly and I was held accountable to have the house tidied so she could clean it every week. That was a great help to me!

Later, I had support in getting my laundry caught up every other week by an older lady from our church. Her sister also came. They helped listen to little children read and taught piano lessons to them for a season. My success in not being overwhelmed leans heavily on not doing it alone, whether it is housework, home education, or skill building. Teamwork works!

Magnify "Christ in you, your hope of glory" in thanksgiving and song daily. Humbly acknowledge your need for His help in prayer, expectant that Jesus wants to, and He will meet your needs in real ways according to His abundant goodness as you trust and obey His leading.

CHAPTER NINE

The Rubber Hits the Road

All this talk about being saintly and whelmed and yoked and abundant and being *with* Jesus sounds good on paper. However, the mark of authenticity is what happens when the rubber hits the road. Every time I've written a study, spoken for a group of people, or presented anything - even if it's the umpteenth time on the same subject - the Lord inevitably allows opportunities for me to put my claims to the test to ensure my authenticity and relatability.

Writing this book is no exception.

I'm writing this chapter after having a routine mammogram last Wednesday. On Friday morning the doctor's office called and said they'd like me to have another mammogram and an ultrasound because I have two spots on my left breast.

I got "that" call. The call where I get to come back for more testing to find out if I have cancer.

They believe one spot is calcification that they'd like to look at more closely. The other spot they deemed a "questionable" mass. They don't know what it is. And since I'm in a high risk category for breast cancer, they made my appointment for right away Monday morning at the hospital clinic and told me to stick around for the results before I go home. Travis will come with me so we will wait and hear the results together.

PRACTICING SURRENDER

Allow me to provide some spiritual context. About a year ago, Travis and I created vision boards. I had taken an e-course on the subject thinking it could be a benefit to my life coaching clients. My board is chock-full of words, phrases and pictures that represent my passions, my callings, my dreams, and my precious family. It is in a beautiful white frame hanging on my bedroom wall, where I can look at it often and pray about what's on it. It represents the things that make me "tick." It's my life summed up within a large white frame.

Last spring I was bowing low before the Lord on my bedroom floor. I sat up and glanced at my vision board and here's what the Holy Spirit washed over me: "Die to all of it."

What? That's the *opposite* of what vision boards are for! I questioned the Lord (okay, "argued" is probably a more accurate word) and felt a distinct call to surrender everything on that board except the section that represented Him. So I looked at each section of the board and placed it on the altar: my husband, my three children, my health, my businesses, my comfort, my hopes for the future... I surrendered it all to Him.

A couple days later our 17-year-old son announced he'd be moving three hours north and living in a 1957 restored camper at his grandparents' house for the summer (and most likely beyond). My youngest baby was moving out already (too premature for my mama's heart). Surrender here meant letting my son go and letting go of what I had pictured for him.

A week or so after that my husband put in his notice at work. He'd been praying about leaving the corporate world and I had been telling him "just wait" (until *I* could feel more financially secure about our future, regardless of how he saw it). He took the plunge to semi-retire in faith, led by the Lord. So I told my Heavenly Father that I trusted Him to guide us and provide for us in ways I couldn't foresee, knowing that He *could*.

A few months after that our daughter got engaged. She would go straight from college (1,000 miles from home) into marriage. Their beautiful engagement was another opportunity for me to surrender by releasing her into her adult life and entrusting her to the Lord and her future husband.

This happened between two epic journeys: one in which my family and I spent about six hours a day for several days doing hard-core hiking in the Andes mountains and tent-camping at night (not my idea of a comfortable, relaxing vacation, though it *was* awesome). The other was to Ghana, Africa, where my husband and I served on a mission base five hours from modern civilization and experientially learned about poverty. I had told the Lord for years how much I valued my comfort. These experiences gave me the opportunity to surrender it.

Surrender, release control, let go, let God. Looking at that vision board, I can see the areas in which my surrender has been tested. Husband: check. Children: check. Comfort: check. Control: check. Travel: check. Knowing what lies ahead: check. Now I get to experience that surrender in relation to my health.

HEALTH: CHECK

I'm at high risk for breast cancer for various reasons. This might not be cancer. *And* there's a good chance it is.

At church this morning I thought, "Well, if it is, will I ask 'Why me, Lord?'" I responded to my own thought. "No, I'll ask, 'Why *not* me?'" Tomorrow morning I will step into this yoke with Jesus, who is already in it with me, and let Him lead. I surrendered my health to Him and this is where the rubber hits the road.

I've done a bit of research about my particular situation so I can be fully informed on whatever is said and done tomorrow. In the process, I've been able to discern my thoughts and feelings on it all. My soul circle feels some fear with a desire to either "fight or flight." My inner spirit/core circle feels peace, joy, and security. It reminds me to face it. The Holy Spirit in me reminds me that we're in this together and that I can hold His hand. I trust Him. I don't need to fight it, run away from it, or ignore it. I will face it. Oh, how I love Him! His promises never fail.

> *Have I not commanded you? Be strong and courageous. Do not be frightened, and do not be dismayed, for the Lord your God is with you wherever you go.* Joshua 1:9
>
> *Fear not, for I am with you; be not dismayed, for I am your God; I will strengthen you, I will help you, I will uphold you with my righteous right hand.* Isaiah 41:10
>
> *Be strong and courageous. Do not fear or be in dread of them, for it is the Lord your God who goes with you. He will not leave you or forsake you.* Deuteronomy 31:6
>
> *The Lord your God is in your midst, a mighty one who will save; he will rejoice over you with gladness; he will quiet you by his love; he will exult over you with loud singing.* Zephaniah 3:17
>
> *...for he has said, "I will never leave you nor forsake you."* Hebrews 13:5b
>
> *For I am sure that neither death nor life, nor angels nor rulers, nor things present nor things to come, nor powers, nor height nor depth, nor anything else in all creation, will be able to separate us from the love of God in Christ Jesus our Lord.* Romans 8:38-39

I am filled with so much of His love and Presence. My soul's fears are still present, but the Lord's Presence in my very core is so much bigger than my fear. He is "rightthere" in this yoke. My health is His. I'm a temple of His Spirit, so this temple belongs to Him.

I've told a handful of people about my upcoming appointments and although I feel trusting and secure in Jesus at my core, I notice my pulse quickens and my voice tightens when I talk about it. Truth be told, I am almost expecting it to be cancer because of my odds and because Jesus knows I will journey with Him through this no matter what.

Another thought flickers through my mind: does the enemy know he cannot defeat me with cancer? That it will only serve to bring me closer to the Lord and proclaim God's praises regardless? That it will actually provide yet another platform where I can declare the goodness of God? I have surrendered my husband and children, my loved ones, my very life to Jesus so if this is the path I walk that brings me home to Him, then I get to entrust all of my life to the Lord - including being absent from it all.

FOCUSING ON A BIG GOD SHRINKS THE ENEMY

I had a short vision a few weeks ago. I turned to my right and faced a non-defined atmosphere that was filled with bright, glorious light. It had no height, depth, or width. I knew it was the essence of God's glory, goodness, and love. When I turned to the left, I saw dark nothingness that seemed to have a defined space but I could not see the edges. I knew this side represented the absence of God: evil.

When I turned to the right again toward the goodness of God, I sensed the darkness to my left getting smaller. I turned to see if that was the case. Indeed it was. As I was looking at the darkness and *thinking* about the light, the darkness continued to become smaller. I decided to face only the bright "God" side and soak it all up! While

I did, I was aware that the darkness on my left became so small that without turning my head from that awesome bright side, I simply lifted the darkness with the top of my left hand and flicked it off with my right hand as if it were a mosquito.

The more enraptured I am with God's essence, the less impact darkness has on me. Was that a vision for how I can face cancer? It certainly provides insight on how to counter threats to my peace and joy. Stay overwhelmed and enthralled with my God and the darkness becomes less relevant. It holds less power. It cannot overwhelm; only God's glory can do that.

TODAY IS THE DAY

Monday...

I slept well last night, thank you, Jesus! Before I get out of bed I say my usual "Thank you Lord for..." and list ten things I am thankful for. I mentally reach for Jesus's hand as I swing my legs out from under the covers and plant my feet on the floor, knowing that this morning is all in His strength and I need Him closely leading me through it. I want to feel the pulse in His hand as I walk through the corridors of the medical center and as I wait in the waiting room.

I calculate how much time I have before we head to the hospital and decide a quick workout will do me some good before my time with the Lord this morning. I can release some nervous energy, get my blood flowing, and since I don't know what to expect today, I would like to appreciate the ability to work out while I can.

My quiet time starts as usual. I read a brief devotional book, another section from another Christian book, and rewrite another chunk of Scripture into my notebook. (I'm copying the book of Nehemiah now.) Then I read a bit from the New Testament before simply soaking in the Lord's Presence.

I pray that His peace comes from deep inside me and I am picturing myself sitting next to Him, shoulder to shoulder, as He wraps His arm around me. Next I see Him directly in front of me, eye-to-eye. He looks at me with love, strength, and compassion and holds out His arms for me to take His hands. I am reminded of the ice-breaker game where one partner gets blindfolded and the "sighted" partner leads the blindfolded partner through an obstacle course while the partners are simply facing each other, holding each other's hands. That is exactly how I feel! Like Jesus is leading me by two hands and I'm blindfolded, but awkward as it is, I trust Him to lead me safely where I need to go.

I will keep my eyes on Him, even when I can't see what's ahead.

Suddenly, the atmosphere in the room shifts. I already feel trust and now I have a heightened sense of joy. I didn't "muster" it, I didn't think of it, and I wasn't looking for it. I'm actually a bit confused. Why do I feel joy? I think of the verse "The joy of the Lord is my strength" (Nehemiah 8:10) and consider the reasons for this sudden shift to joy.

Maybe my results will be the best case scenario and I'm already feeling the joy that will come in a few hours. Maybe I have cancer and the Lord will heal me down the road, which will also elicit joy. Or maybe I have cancer and the joy of the Lord will sustain my faith through the tough journey ahead. I decide the reason for my current joy is irrelevant at the moment and I can simply let it overflow from me rather than figure it out. I am not overwhelmed by my circumstances because peace, trust, and joy is whelming from within me.

I take a deep breath and get ready to go. I am surprisingly calm despite a few random thoughts that sneak in. "Maybe this is why your husband retired early. So he can take care of you." "How will you tell your parents you have cancer?" Interesting how these thoughts are "you" and not "I." These are not my thoughts. These are the enemy's plants.

I choose joy.

I figuratively turn to the right and face the glorious Light, flicking the darkness off my hand. I am ready to face whatever lies ahead and I feel peace.

SURRENDERED AND READY TO FACE IT

We check in at the Breast Center. Travis goes to the regular waiting area and I head back to a separate area where all of us wearing lovely oversized pink tops get to hang out while we wait for tests and results. I have no idea what to expect, other than what two people have warned me: that the worst part in all of this is the waiting room and that I should give myself permission to go into a changing room or bathroom to cry out my fear and frustration. I marvel at that for a moment because I don't feel overwhelmed by my emotions - at least not yet - so I sit next to a gal who looks about my age. Heck, if we're both here, we've got something in common.

I decide *not* to follow social protocol by remaining silent and protecting privacy and all that. Instead, I say, "Hey, we both look pretty cute in our tops don't we?" Her conceding smile is enough to warrant my next question. "Are you here for a routine exam or is this something extra?" "Both," she says. Turns out we are there for the exact same reason, getting the exact same tests. "Do you have someone here with you?" I say. She's flying solo for this so I tell her, "Well, I'm here with you," and smile. She chuckles gratefully and gets called in for her exam.

While I wait, not yet knowing my fate, one by one various women come into the waiting room and out again. I speak to all of them and get to hear stories ranging from "routine exam" to "diagnosed in '06 and went through…" I'm grateful for all these women, each of them shining in their own way. We're all a little uncomfortable, some of us are a bit overwhelmed, and some are matter-of-fact. I decide it's a real blessing to choose joy when I can share it with people despite our circumstances.

THE TESTS

The mammogram tech is friendly and highly skilled. She takes a bajillion awkward, uncomfortable, and sometimes downright painful x-rays and escorts me back to the waiting room. I text a picture of myself in my pretty pink shirt to Travis, who is not allowed in this waiting room.

I had anticipated that Travis and I would go through this together and hear the results together, but I see that it will be just me and Jesus walking through this lab work and hearing the results. Okay, I'm choosing to lean in. I'm facing it with my Creator. He's got me.

Then it's time for the ultrasound and fortunately, this tech is also comforting and skillful. As I look at the screen she sees during the procedure, I watch her repeatedly measure a (seemingly) large mass from various angles. For a long time. Watching this is fascinating, but because I know she could be measuring a malignant mass, I decide to look away and focus on Jesus leading me down this shared journey. I want to face His Light right now rather than contemplate the darkness and stir up fear and anxiety.

The technician excuses herself from the room to go get the doctor, which leaves me alone with my thoughts and with the Lord. Because I am pillow-wedged onto one side of my back, I imagine that I'm leaning on Jesus. I remember the verse, "You hem me in behind and before" (Psalm 139:5). He is hemming me in on all sides! He is right here with me. I breathe deeply and exhale slowly, realizing I am minutes away from an answer. Do I have cancer? Is that the path I'll be walking? I am prepared and I am at peace. I am surrendered. The joy of the Lord is my strength.

The ultrasound technician and the doctor come back in. He introduces himself and proceeds to do the exam while scrutinizing the screen. I feel like somehow time is standing still and I could probably hear a pin drop. Like this whole experience is somehow suspended in space and time. I'm staring at his face, looking for a sign. He and the technician exchange a few non-emotive words that I can't interpret and then he turns to face me. I look him in the eyes, ready. I have my two questions prepared for when he speaks. (I'll ask him what *exactly* I'm dealing with and what my next step is.)

THE VERDICT

The doctor steadily returns my eye contact and says, "One of these areas is simply calcification, which is benign. The other is a mass that appears to be a cyst that has gotten larger since your last mammogram. We saw it on your previous one and it has changed so we wanted to take a closer look. It's benign. There's no sign of cancer in your breast."

I do not have cancer.

I lay there stunned for a moment, letting that sink in. I was so prepared to face it that the idea of no cancer is taking awhile to absorb. Finally, I fire a bunch of probing questions at him just to make sure and then I smile wide, satisfied with his answers. When he leaves, the technician and I exchange smiles and I say, "It's the best possible result."

My appointments are done so I get changed, exit the now-*full*-of-pink-shirted-women waiting room, and find Travis. I'm so happy to share the news with him that cancer is not the path we will be walking. Praise Jesus!

Later Monday night…

The last several days have been a bit of a blur. There have been many opportunities to take my thoughts captive and to test how much I have truly surrendered my life. I am so relieved and thankful about my diagnosis and I recognize this as an opportunity to see how I deal with could-be overwhelm that became an opportunity for overflow in the midst of writing this book.

And you experienced it with me.

I walked out of the hospital today feeling as though something had lifted. I wanted to shout from the mountain tops how thankful I was. Instead, Travis and I ended up running errands. It was just another day. I went through the motions of "just another day" while internally busting at the seams with gratitude: overflowing, abundant gratitude. I'll take "just another day!"

Last night someone at a meeting prayed for me and said she saw me as a tree with large, deep roots. On my way home from that meeting, I pictured myself as that tree in the midst of a storm, damaged and broken, yet still standing, rooted and anchored in Christ.

We are pressed on all sides, but not crushed; perplexed, but not in despair; persecuted, but not forsaken; struck down, but not destroyed. 2 Corinthians 4:8-9

If I am pressed on all sides, but not crushed, I have strength. If I am perplexed but not in despair, I have peace. If I am persecuted but not forsaken, I have trust. If I am struck down but not destroyed, I have perseverance. We all have these qualities of strength, peace, trust, and perseverance in our core - in our root system - when we know Jesus as our Savior.

WHELMING WITH GRATITUDE

Tuesday…

It has been a full 24 hours since I learned that my mystery mass is benign. In my time with the Lord this morning, I sat in my comfy chair and began reading my little devotional book as usual. When I reached for my next book, I was so *overwhelmed by gratitude* and the need to praise the Lord that I simply went to the floor and spent (who knows how much) time in whelming worship. My overwhelming gratitude caused my heart to overflow. I had the song "He is Worthy of it All" in my head and heart and declared to Jesus how much He is truly worthy of my praise, my devotion, and indeed, my whole life.

After a long while I looked up at my vision board as I have so many times before. I realized that it's not just surrendered, it's dedicated. It's consecrated. My life is completely lost and found in Him because He is worthy of it all - whether I'm flying high with Jesus or whether the rubber is hitting the road and we're journeying together down an unexpected path. A path where I can abide with Him, fully whelmed.

For Reflection and Regeneration

1. Think about areas of your life (other than your faith) that you are unwilling to give up.

   a. Why are you unwilling to surrender those?

   b. Identify the underlying fear that causes you to cling to that part of your life.

2. Create a list of everything in your life that you deem relevant. (What/who consumes your time, thoughts, energy, commitments...?)

   a. After you've created your list, start at the top and decide if it's something you can control. If you can control any part of it, put a check next to it.

   b. Look at the items you checked. Imagine scooping those list items (and all they represent) into your hands and forming a ball with them. Now imagine yourself with Jesus, tightly grasping your control ball. Then open your hands, release your control ball, and give it to Jesus. Do this mentally *and* spiritually.

3. Across the entire list write in large letters, "Property of Jesus."

KELLY GIRARD

A Fully Whelmed Tornado Devastation Testimony

On a Sunday evening, my husband and I decided to forego our usual coffee date because the weather was questionable. Where we live in the South, a tornado watch normally wouldn't change our plans, but this day was considered a high danger for strong tornadoes. Shortly after 7 pm, we received multiple address-specific tornado warnings. Looking out the front window, we were able to see the storm and knew it was the real thing, and it was coming toward us.

Thankfully we had always taken warnings seriously, so our family knew the drill. Dogs, rabbit, lizard, medications, a few cherished items, and eight people - all into the master closet, which the original homeowners had built as a safe room. In minutes we took a direct hit from a huge, violent tornado. It was absolutely terrifying. While our family survived, others lost their lives that night. Our home, vehicles, everything - destroyed or gone altogether. Our neighborhood was a disaster zone that I can't even describe.

The days and months that followed were incredibly difficult. I was grateful for God's goodness to us, yet raw and hurting from the loss of our life as it had been, as well as the trauma of the experience itself. Every morning when I woke up in the rental house, my first thought *and prayer was, "God, I don't want to do this day." The kids could feed themselves, but the dogs needed to be walked, and that is what got me out of bed. Many days I couldn't even figure out what to do - the tasks toward rebuilding, replacing, and recovering were overwhelming. At first I felt if I had enough faith, I wouldn't be hurting so much, but then I went to Scripture and read Job. I saw that Job suffered. He trusted God, but he felt the pain of his circumstances. I understood that faith doesn't mean denying the hurt; it means trusting God in the midst of it.*

I need other people. When I couldn't take another step, my friends stepped in. When I was at my limit, I needed my friends to help me. This was God's overflow. The day after the tornado, an acquaintance called and said, "I need to do something to help you. Please give me something to do!" I said, "Ok, my daughter's birthday is in three days, and we have nothing." She rallied her friends, many who did not even know us, went shopping, and delivered a wonderful birthday party when I had barely slept in days and couldn't think straight. It blessed our family tremendously, and allowed her the blessing of giving. In so many ways, we would not have made it without the many people who came alongside us in our need. Allow others to help you.

God's faithfulness, strength, and provision do not depend on my faith performance. No matter how I feel, Jesus feels just fine. God's grace is sufficient in my weakness. In the most difficult days, I was not having in-depth Bible study or lengthy prayers. I was weak. But God is faithful. He holds onto you when you can't hold onto Him.

Each day has enough trouble of its own. One day at a time. One step at a time. When there is too much to do, ask God what He has for you that day. Then don't worry about everything else.

Trusting God and knowing His joy and comfort does not mean all pain and overwhelmed feelings disappear. They can co-exist and this is okay. I think this is part of seeing God's presence and power when we face our difficult circumstances. I may still have fears and feel overwhelmed, but I trust that God is bigger, and my hope is in Him.

Two verses encouraged my family during this time.

2 Corinthians 6:10 - "...as sorrowful, yet always rejoicing..."

This was the validation that we can be grieving yet grateful at the same time - exactly what we were experiencing.

2 Corinthians 5:1 "For we know that if the tent that is our earthly home is destroyed, we have a building from God, a house not made with hands, eternal in the heavens." This one kept our focus on the eternal rather than our current situation.

CHAPTER TEN

Say to This Mountain...

*"Have faith in God," Jesus answered. "Truly I tell you, if anyone
says to this mountain, 'Go, throw yourself into the sea,' and does not
doubt in their heart but believes that what they say will happen,
it will be done for them. Therefore I tell you, whatever you ask for
in prayer, believe that you have received it, and it will be yours."*
Mark 11:22-24

Words have power. They are instrumental in our shift from overwhelm to overflow.

Remember the old chant, "Sticks and stones will break my bones but words will never hurt me?" On the contrary, words have the power to inflict pain that we hold onto far longer than a physical injury.

However, words can also speak life and healing! They can lift a person's spirits, provide comfort, and glorify God. Words we choose in the midst of overwhelm will either declare defeat or they will declare the love and power of God.

So what do you declare in the midst of overwhelm?

What we say is important because words carry power. They can drastically impact our environment. Consider that God used words to create the whole world! Recall Genesis 1 where the phrase "and God said" occurs repeatedly.

"God said…" and the universe, our earth, and all that *is* was formed. Those were some powerful words from a powerful God.

In addition, Jesus is the embodiment of God's Word. He was God's Word of creation.

*In the beginning was the **Word**, and the **Word** was with God, and the **Word** was God. He was with God in the beginning. Through him all things were made; without him nothing was made that has been made.* John 1:1-3

There are so many verses in the Bible about God's Word. Check out 1 Samuel 3:21, Psalm 107:20, Psalm 119:105, Isaiah 55:11, Matthew 4:4, Matthew 8:8, John 17:17, and Hebrews 4:12 for a small sampling.

Okay, we get that God's Word is important and powerful, but how about ours? Here are some verses that tell us about the importance and power of the words we speak.

THE SIGNIFICANCE OF OUR WORDS

*The Spirit of the LORD spoke through me; his **word** was on **my tongue**.* 2 Samuel 23:2

*Anxiety weighs down the heart, but a kind **word** cheers it up.* Proverbs 12:25

*The soothing **tongue** is a tree of life, but a perverse **tongue** crushes the spirit.* Proverbs 15:4

*A good man brings good things out of the good stored up in his heart, and an evil man brings evil things out of the evil stored up in his heart. For the mouth **speaks** what the heart is full of.* Luke 6:45

*If you **declare** with your mouth, "Jesus is Lord," and believe in your heart that God raised him from the dead, you will be saved.* Romans 10:9

*The **tongue** has the power of life and death, and those who love it will eat its fruit.* Proverbs 18:21

Did you catch that last one? The tongue has the power of life and death!

It's not about "thinking happy thoughts." It's about focusing on the goodness of God rather than on the schemes of the enemy, who wants to bring us down.

The thief comes only to steal and kill and destroy. I came that they may have life and have it abundantly. John 10:10 (ESV)

So when we're in the midst of overwhelming circumstances, we can choose words that will declare defeat or words that will declare victory in Christ.

Will we declare a victory for the "thief" or will we declare the Lord's victory?

And to whom or to what are we making these declarations, anyway?

To God.

To ourselves.

To other people.

To the universe (basically everything and everyone).

CHOOSING OUR WORDS

Check out these two lists. Which list declares victory in Christ and hope for the future?

I give up.	I'm giving this to You, God.
I can't do this.	I can do all things through Christ who strengthens me (Phil 4:13).
I'm drained.	Fill me up, Lord.
There's too much on my plate.	God is bigger than my plate.
This will never change.	God's able to do more than I could ask or imagine.
God's not listening to me.	God's ways and His timing are perfect.
I am invisible.	I am God's masterpiece (Eph 2:10).
I'm going to lose my mind.	I have the mind of Christ (1 Cor. 2:16).
I'm fearful.	The courage in my spirit is bigger than the fear in my soul.
This is impossible.	All things are possible with God.
I'm terrible at...	I'm working on...
I'm failing.	I'm learning.

When we become aware of our defeated language, we are empowered to choose something different; to choose words that will bring life rather than defeat.

FOR EXAMPLE...

Consider the following hypothetical scene with Tom and Terese, whose son Joey has been in a self-induced crisis which is wreaking havoc on their home life. Notice what each parent is declaring in the midst of the trial.

Tom: I can't keep going on like this. Joey's issues are too much for me. I need a break. Why doesn't he just get help? Where's God in all this? We're going to end up losing him and go bankrupt in the process. It's hopeless. He'll never change.

Terese: Tom, you've been a failure as a father, so why do you care now? Why does it always have to be about you? You'll never change either. This is tearing us apart and we'll end up getting a divorce. He won't get better and our lives will be miserable regardless of Joey.

Notice all the defeated declarations Tom and Terese make? Their words reveal souls filled with anger, fear, hopelessness, victim thinking, and blame. They're both using language that proclaims with certainty a future of misery and isolation for themselves. Their declarations align with the purposes of the enemy: "to steal, kill, and destroy."

Maybe you've heard the phrase, "What you focus on you find." If we focus on our overwhelming sense of defeat and declare it, we'll surely find it. If Tom and Terese continue to declare these things for their son and each other now and in the future, they will most likely come to pass.

Since words are powerful, let's use them to declare something better. Something that's life-giving and hopeful. Something that aligns with what God wants for us.

Here's an alternative scene for Tom and Terese.

Tom: It's so hard to see Joey this way. I'm feeling frustrated and tired and I don't know how we're going to make ends meet through this. But I know that God is good and somehow He's got this. He's got us. The only thing we can do is pray for Joey. Please, Terese, can we pray together for him? Jesus is our only hope in all this.

Terese: It's been tough on our marriage too. I feel like I'm crying all the time. I do want to pray with you. We need each other and we need Jesus. I don't know what the future holds, but I know that if we keep praying, we'll get through it together and be there for Joey.

In this scene, Tom and Terese still verbalize the emotions they're experiencing. But instead of a defeated, hopeless, and attacking overwhelm, they speak their surrender (acknowledgment) of what *is* and declare the goodness and faithfulness of God in the midst of it. This hope in the Lord serves to unify them rather than tear them apart. It draws their attention to the goodness of God instead of imploding into themselves and exploding onto each other.

When Tom and Terese use their words to focus on the Lord in the midst of their overwhelm, they'll find Him. When they declare their abundant hope in Christ, it deflates the schemes of the enemy to steal, kill, and destroy their relationship with the Lord and with each other.

Since words are so powerful, it follows that we would desire to use them to declare God's goodness in any situation, right? To "wax eloquent" to the universe even in the direst of circumstances.

CONTROLLED BY EMOTIONS VS.
EXPRESSING EMOTIONS

Truth be told, sometimes my words have looked less like victorious declarations and more like rapid-fire "verbal vomit."

Sometimes I've been so overwhelmed I've felt like a balloon expanding with stress, stretching until the air inside either rushed out or caused the balloon to pop. If you've ever blown up a balloon and released it before tying the end, you've observed the expelling air propel the balloon wildly through the air until it became flat again. It's a chaotic scene.

And relatable.

A number of years ago I felt such overwhelming, defeated stress from my circumstances that my husband would come home from work, take one look at my face, and announce to our kids, "I'm going to go 'walk the mom.'" We'd venture out into the neighborhood so I could expel my thoughts and feelings wildly; hands gesturing my exasperation and desperation, adrenaline-fueled legs pumping quickly up the neighborhood hills, and tongue spewing forth the frustrations of my situation. Once my emotions were verbally vomited we returned home.

Many days my husband wasn't able to "walk the mom." Then I was more like a balloon that gets blown up and instead of tying the end, you pinch it between your fingers to let a tiny bit of air out so that it produces a high-pitched squeal. My pent-up emotions were kept under wraps just enough for my children to see my pinched expressions, hear my terse language, and experience some squeaks of frustration that escaped from my mouth enough to reveal what was in my heart.

I was trying to stuff how I felt (swallow my words) in my desperation to vent, which was consuming, frustrating, and exhausting. It only added to my overwhelm.

Really, those seasons reflected my lack of intimacy with the Lord and my desire to have life look like I thought it should. My relationship with Him consisted of a quick Bible-reading followed by a short prayer, telling Jesus to fix the situation. I did not seek *Him* as much as I sought His solution to my problem. I wasn't surrendered to Him as much as I was desperate to tell Him (or my husband, my friends, or prayer partners) how unhappy the situation made me.

When my soul is depleting and nothing of spiritual value is filling it, my *reactive emotions* reflect the overwhelm of my heart. However, when I'm whelming with Jesus's Spirit, I can acknowledge my natural, human emotions, and reflect *Him*.

FULLY HUMAN AND FULLY SURRENDERED

When He overflows in us, whether we're sad, angry, or ecstatic, our reactions and our language will demonstrate both our humanness and our relationship with the Lord simultaneously. Jesus's experience as a human expressing emotions (i.e. John 11:35: "Jesus wept") means that I am fully human when I feel and express emotions, and His experience as the sinless second person of the Trinity means that what I do with those emotions reveals my sin or my surrender in the circumstance.

Verbal vomit does not need to be my main outlet to deal with overwhelming circumstances in my life. The more present I am with Jesus in any given moment the less I find myself needing to either erupt from the mouth or bite my tongue 'till it hurts.

When I am surrendered, I am emptied of *myself*: my need for justification, for sympathy, for control, for attention, and for being right. In that place of emptying myself and surrendering all those things, I can express my emotions *and* be an open vessel for the Lord to pour into me until I overflow with Him.

Plus, I'm discovering my mouth feels a lot better without my foot stuck in it.

Yes, I get frustrated, disappointed, angry, sad, and every other human emotion there is. However, rather than "pitching a fit" with an emotional explosion or a series of phrases that promulgate defeat, I'm working toward being continually grounded enough in Christ to simultaneously *experience and surrender* my emotions to Him. Being in that state enables me to choose words that focus on Christ rather than on doom and gloom.

SAY TO THIS MOUNTAIN...

Look at what Jesus said about the power of a believer's words.

"...for truly I say to you, if you have faith the size of a mustard seed, **you will say to this mountain***, 'Move from here to there,' and it will move; and nothing will be impossible to you."* Matthew 17:20

Jesus replied, "Truly I tell you, if you have faith and do not doubt, not only can you do what was done to the fig tree, but also **you can say to this mountain***, 'Go, throw yourself into the sea,' and it will be done."* Matthew 21:21

"Have faith in God," Jesus answered. "Truly I tell you, if **anyone says to this mountain***, 'Go, throw yourself into the sea,' and does not doubt in their heart but believes that what they say will happen, it will be done for them. Therefore I tell you, whatever you ask for in prayer, believe that you have received it, and it will be yours.* Mark 11:22-24

So what is your mountain?

A relationship? Finances? A big goal? An event? Your health? A life change? An overwhelming trial? Surrender it to the God of the universe. Have faith in *Him* rather than placing your faith in the results of your situation. Allow God's goodness and love to pour into you. And face that mountain.

Then choose what you want to say to the mountain. Choose what you declare to God, yourself, and others about it. Declare the victory of Christ in your life in any circumstance, and notice what whelms in you.

Because when it comes to shifting from overwhelm to overflow, words matter.

For Reflection and Regeneration

1. What are some words or phrases you've used that reflect defeat?

2. What are some words or phrases you can use to replace those?

3. Read 2 Corinthians 11:16-33. (Paul is writing "tongue-in-cheek" here).

   a. Has Paul had reason to feel overwhelmed by his circumstances?

   b. How do we know Paul lived from overflow? (Hint: read what Paul wrote in 1 Thessalonians 5:16-18.)

4. Try this litmus test for 24 hours. Any words that you think or speak, add "Lord Jesus" after them. Can you say His Name and feel at peace about the words that preceded it?

5. Our words reveal our heart. Read some verses from God's Word that reveal God's heart toward you. Write your favorites on notecards and refer to them often.

   a. Psalm 18:19
   b. Romans 8:38-39
   c. 1 John 3:1a
   d. John 17:23
   e. Eph. 5:29
   f. 1 Peter 2:9

6. What is a current mountain in your life?

   a. What can you say to that mountain?
   b. Do your words reflect defeat or hope in Christ?

ANDREA FOX

A Fully Whelmed Home-life Turmoil Testimony

Five years ago, I was spiritually anemic, physically drained, emotionally spent, mentally overwhelmed, and so, so, so lonely. Over time, despite the best of intentions, I had put the needs and wants of others so far beyond my own that I didn't know who I was anymore, and I didn't even know what my own needs were or how to meet them. I was drowning in all that I was trying to manage and I couldn't figure out how in the world I was going to get out of it.

During my college years I met a wonderful man. We fell in love and were married one month after I graduated. Over the next 15 years, I neglected my spiritual needs and I was completely and utterly empty. I chose to live on lonely shame, because my pastor husband was an alcoholic.

I thought this was so unfair, and my anger seethed behind closed doors. I would yell at him to fight his alcohol addiction. Our young boys would emulate me by yelling at my husband disrespectfully when they had conflict with him. When he was overbearing with the boys, when they had conflict, or when their relationship seemed militant, I would jump in like an interpreter. I would take things too personally, too seriously, and value reactions of others as my self-worth.

Overwhelmed at all I was handling at the time, I told him I wanted out of the church we were at. I simply said I wasn't going any more to be "on display" for him to look good. This was a daunting sign for our marriage, and only the tip of my deepest moment of overwhelm.

Then, my mother-in-law shot and murdered my father-in-law and committed suicide. The shock of the news was flattening and snatched my breath away. Dealing with media and all the details of the estate was suffocating. My grief was mixed with rage that she had controlled my life once again. I had started graduate school one semester earlier, and I chose to have a leave of absence to handle the hurricane of decisions. After all, this was the pattern I had set up in our marriage where I handle everything tough.

My husband's addiction spun to a new level, his rage deepened, and his verbal abuse escalated. I knew we needed help, and following the advice of a trusted pastor's wife, we sought therapy. While in counseling, my husband admitted pornography addiction all throughout our marriage. Afraid of being hurt more, my caretaking kicked up, and I began checking his internet history and phone. This only added to the crazy in my mind, and overwhelm took on a deeper level that I did not know existed.

He was considering going away to treatment, and he would dangle that carrot in front of me, threatening me that he might not go. I chose to act like I was indifferent, just so he didn't have that power over me. It was a terrifying time, because I would hold my breath each day with his rage, hoping and wishing he would just go away. I didn't fully relax until I knew he had checked in.

He was gone for 4 months, and I was essentially a single mom in addition to the quarterback for the estate details. I was filled with loneliness, shame, fear, and grief. I had PTSD from his pornography addiction disclosure as well as the murder suicide. I remember staring at myself in the mirror in disbelief, thinking, "I'm that woman," knowing that I had many reasons to support a divorce. The realization that I was "one of those people" often caused me to be in a stunned state; it was too much to handle. With all the stress I had faced, I simply chose not to make any major decisions for our relationship.

Being able to relax and think about my needs with him gone, I chose to reach out in all directions for help. I joined Bible studies and support groups. Within the course of two weeks, God gave me a new verse from three different places. "So do not throw away this confident trust in the Lord. Remember the great reward it brings you! Patient endurance is what you need now, so that you will continue to do all God's will. Then you will receive all that he has promised." Hebrews 10:35-36.

I connected to Celebrate Recovery, found acceptance, and found that I could at last be authentic, broken, and honest with my disappointments. Then music spoke to me so deeply, and I saw people that had been through real pain, yet they had a rock solid strength that I wanted. I completed a step study and trusted the process. Jeremiah 6:14 says "You can't heal a wound by saying it's not there!" The first principle was big for me because I always knew that I was not God. However, I didn't realize that every time I thought I knew how someone else should run their life, I was acting like I thought I was God.

It struck me how although I had already turned my life over to God, I needed to continually turn my will over to him daily. James 5:16 says "Therefore confess your sins to each other and pray for each other so that you may be healed." I was surprised by the healing of sharing my life story. I went to counseling and as my therapist said, God began building a new spine in me, one vertebra at time.

Through recovery, I am freed to release the shame of my husband's addictions. I learned I don't need to fight other people's battles, I'm not God, and I don't need to control outcomes. I learned to look at my actions and question myself if they were coming from a root of control or safety. I learned how to have boundaries, and to let God do his work in others in His timing.

In recovery, I learned that my anger was due to unresolved resentments, which were due to expectations. Because of Jesus Christ giving me grace for my sins and imperfections, I can give grace and love to others. Having completed an in-home separation and lots of counseling, my husband and I continue to work the steps, and God has healed our marriage with a new and deeper intimacy than before. In Christ, I am able to walk others through their recovery by being a step study leader, sponsor, and back up vocalist.

I choose to live a quality-driven life, in a BEingness into which I know Christ has called me. By seeking out personal development, keeping my tap roots deep in God, hearing Him through the Spirit, and following Jesus' call on my life, I grow closer to Him. My husband is on the same path of growth, and as a result our intimacy is healed.

Five years ago I heard kind, encouraging people saying that it would take three to five years to heal our marriage with both of us working at it. At the time, I couldn't even imagine getting through the next five minutes. As 2 Peter 1:5 says, "For this very reason, make every effort to supplement your faith with virtue, and virtue with knowledge, and knowledge with self-control, and self-control with steadfastness, and stead-fastness with godliness, and godliness with brotherly affection, and brotherly affection with love." Friends, continue the path of healing. As a cruise ship turns slowly over time without the passengers noticing, you will notice the change in your life over time if you stay the course.

Philippians 3:13- 14, "I do not consider that I have made it my own. But one thing I do: forgetting what lies behind and straining forward to what lies ahead, I press on toward the goal for the prize of the upward call of God in Christ Jesus." With skilled therapists, I have felt heard, and I have understood the source of all these unhealthy patterns in our lives. I have forgiven my mother-in-law, my husband, and myself. I am thankful for the overwhelming situations that were the impetus of choosing to face pain, and as a result be fully filled with Christ.

To the reader that can't see the way to get to a place of strength, that feels like no one else has their struggle, that is in dismay and disbelief of the future, that is weighed down in shame, that feels they have to hold it all together, that feels they can't hold it all together, that wonders if God sees their struggle, that feels like to object of public scrutiny, you are not alone and healing is possible. Choose a new path, claim His truths and trust Christ to recover.

Indeed, 2 Corinthians 5:17 says "Therefore, if anyone is in Christ, he is a new creation. The old has passed away, behold the new has come."

CHAPTER ELEVEN

Allegory of the Cave

Plato had his "Allegory of the Cave." I've got one too. Nestle in for another multi-part vision. I recall this one nearly as frequently as the hamster cage vision.

In part one, I walk into a cave that is nestled on a high ledge overlooking a city. Scanning the walls, I notice immediately they are lined with gemstones of various sizes and colors. The gems are beautiful and bountiful and I am in awe.

My hand reaches out to a palm-sized red gem and without thinking about it, I pluck the gem out of the wall. Instantly, another red gem grows back in its place. It dawns on me that if I take this gem out to the people of the city and do some good with it, I can come back to the cave and get more. I don't need to hoard any because the gems are abundant and replenish themselves. I run out of the cave, excited to use the value of the gem to serve people, knowing that I can come back and get more.

INDEPENDENT SERVICE

In the second part of the vision, I walk into the cave with the recent experience of plucking the first gem fresh on my mind. I realize I can do this again and it is fulfilling to know I'm helping others. This time I examine how the gems are set into the cave walls. Some gems are small enough to pick out with my thumb and index finger. Other gems could fit in the palm of my hand, and still others look so huge I'm sure I couldn't pull them out and carry them.

I decide to try a bigger gem than last time, bracing myself for a greater effort to pluck it out. I'm surprised that it comes out easily. I then realize that whatever sized gem I'm ready for will be just the right weight for me to lift - not too heavy and not too light, not too big or too small. The size and weight of the gem I pluck is directly proportional to my capacity to use it.

When I'm in the cave again after investing another gem in the people of the city, it occurs to me that I'm doing Kingdom work by bringing these gems out to the people in Jesus's Name and ministering to them with the gems' value.

And I have not consulted Jesus about it.

I've simply grabbed the gems and gone. I look around toward the back of the cave and see that there's a throne with Jesus sitting on it. This is His throne room!

I approach His throne, desiring to acknowledge Him, worship Him, and consult Him about the gems. I am stepping into being more Mary-like by being *with* Jesus now. My cave experience up to this point was more Martha-like; doing *for* Jesus. The other two gems did a world of good, and yet in my Martha-ness I may have missed an even greater opportunity for the Lord.

(Geesh. All this teaching from the Lord about yokes and hamster wheels and being "Mare-tha" and I still jumped right into the action without consulting the Director. I am a work in progress.)

Back at His throne, I'm in awe. He's so calm and peaceful and loving and gracious even after I walked right in here, snatched His gems from His throne room, and ran out with them. I get the sense that He knows me so well, He knew I'd eventually come to Him. Oh, how I appreciate His grace!

I bow before His throne for a bit and afterwards, I am ready to pluck a gem. He didn't tell me exactly which gem to pluck and yet I am comfortable going for a big one, knowing I have His blessing and His encouragement. And it won't be too heavy or too big and awkward.

USING GOD'S KINGDOM TREASURES WITH HIM

In the third installment of this vision, I return from the city and enter the cave-throne room again. I immediately beeline it for Jesus, passing all the gorgeous gemstones glistening from the walls.

The fact that I can even walk into this place amazes me! That I can enter the throne room and head right over to the throne and there's Jesus welcoming me. It's like He's been waiting for me all along. He and I spend some time together and then I'm ready to go to the gemstones.

This time before plucking one out of the wall I have another realization. I don't want to run out of the cave with it immediately. I want to bring it back to the throne and present it to Jesus first.

I gently grasp a beautiful sparkling gem, bring it back to the throne, and see Jesus beaming at me. We are doing this together. Everything I have is from Him, through Him, to Him, for Him, and with Him. Even as I'm carrying the gem into the city, I'm carrying Him with me.

On that day you will realize that I am in my Father, and you are in me, and I am in you. John 14:20

I am the vine; you are the branches. If you remain in me and I in you, you will bear much fruit; John 15:5a

That's where the vision ended.

And where my new understanding of my Christian life began.

Recall the three circles. The cave represents the spirit, that inner core circle. When Christ is our Lord and Savior, He sits on the throne in our inner core. He has lavished us with treasure from Heaven. In my vision, that treasure was represented with abundant, continually renewing gemstones that were more beautiful and plentiful than anything I'd seen. The treasure our Lord bestows on us in our innermost being is from Him, through Him, to Him, for Him, and with Him. He entrusts us with it.

In my vision, using the gemstones required my willing and active participation in what the Lord had for me. He's not interested in my passivity. He wants me to *use* those gemstones - my resources, my energy, my gifts and talents - for His Kingdom because they're from Him and because His intention is for them (for me) to bear fruit. And because He is God, He has an abundant, endless supply for me to use. Nothing that comes from Him is *too* heavy or *too* light.

A BIBLICAL EXAMPLE

For it will be like a man going on a journey, who called his servants and entrusted to them his property. To one he gave five talents, to another two, to another one, to each according to his ability. Then he went away. He who had received the five talents went at once and traded with them, and he made five talents more. So also he who had the two talents made two talents more. But he who had received the one talent went and dug in the ground and hid his master's money. Now after a long time the master of those servants came and settled accounts with them. And he who had received the five talents came forward, bringing five talents more, saying, 'Master, you delivered to me five talents; here, I have made five talents more.' His master said to him, 'Well done, good and faithful servant. You have been faithful over a little; I will set you over much. Enter into the joy of your master.' And he also who had the two talents came forward, saying, 'Master, you delivered to me two talents; here, I have made two talents more.' His master said to him, 'Well done, good and faithful servant. You have been faithful over a little; I will set you over much. Enter into the joy of your master.' He also who had received the one talent came forward, saying, 'Master, I knew you to be a hard man, reaping where you did not sow, and gathering where you scattered no seed, so I was afraid, and I went and hid your talent in the ground. Here, you have what is yours.' But his master answered him, 'You wicked and slothful servant! You knew that I reap where I have not sown and gather where I scattered no seed? Then you ought to have invested my money with the bankers, and at my coming I should have received what was my own with interest. So take the talent from him and give it to him who has the ten talents. For to everyone who has will more be given, and he will have an abundance. But from the one who has not, even what he has will be taken away.

Matthew 25:14-30 (ESV)

In this parable, the talents were given to the servants by their master. He expected them to do something with them; to produce "fruit" with them. Notice that the servants who were given five talents and two talents doubled their investment. Their master knew how much they could handle and was pleased when they produced fruit.

Then there was that third servant who only received one talent. Apparently just that one talent was overwhelming for him. When he buried it, it was a display of his defeated overwhelm. Perhaps the master knew the servant was prone to overwhelm, and entrusting him with just one talent was his way of showing grace by empowering this servant with another opportunity to bear fruit.

And he blew it.

Not because he didn't have the resources or the opportunity to use them, but because his fear was bigger than his hope.

We all have the capability to walk into Jesus's glorious cave. When our inner spirit is His throne room, we are not hopelessly overwhelmed, burying opportunities due to our fear. God's resources are unlimited, His grace is sufficient, His love is eternal, and His ability to empower us to bear fruit for Him is inevitable when we abide in Him (John 15:4-5).

OTHER CAVE SCENARIOS

Some people choose not to enter that "Jesus" cave at all. They choose a different cave that is without Jesus. They want to create their own treasure. They'll find gems in that non-Jesus cave, but they are limited in size, number, and luster, and there is no way to tell if any of them are too big or too small until they're carrying them. Once they are plucked, the gems are not replaced. These people can become overwhelmed easily because their identity is dependent on what they do with the gems and how many they have. Consequently, their efforts are never quite enough. They feel as though *they* are never enough.

Some people enter Jesus's cave, admire the gemstones, and do nothing with them. They figure someone else with more unction can do something with those gems because the work to mine them and any subsequent actions with the gems seems overwhelming. It's easier to go back to the city and simply receive from the stones others will bring to them. Once they've left the cave and gone to the city, they might peak into the cave once in awhile to see if Jesus is still there or not, but mining those gemstones looks like too much work and too much responsibility. The overwhelm sends them back to the city empty-handed, only able to take from others.

Some people use Jesus's cave treasures without acknowledging that He owns it all in the first place. They might be dedicated humanitarians, gifted musicians, incredible solution finders, talented artists, extraordinary designers, intellectual geniuses, or generous givers, yet they do not acknowledge the Giver of their gifts. They miss out on glorifying God and instead, receive glory for themselves. They whelm with independence and therefore, can be easily overwhelmed by a fear of failure.

Others enter the cave but are too afraid to approach His throne and interact with Him for fear of judgment or rejection and believe they can interact with the Lord only if they *perform* well enough with the gemstones . They believe their works are what make them worthy to interact with Him and can easily become overwhelmed in their striving.

This perspective doesn't take into account that Jesus already did it all on the cross and *He* makes us worthy of God's love and acceptance based on *His* merits - not ours.

Others "play small," only picking and using the tiniest of stones without trusting the Lord to empower them to handle the bigger ones. All the while there is an endless supply ready and waiting with Jesus right there - also ready and waiting. They live a life of *under*whelm for fear of doing it "wrong" or of being hurt. By avoiding the bigger stones - the bigger opportunities - they miss out on the bigger blessings for themselves, others, and God.

When we're overflowing, we're using His abundant gemstones with joy, gratitude, and generosity.

Acknowledge Jesus as the King of your soul. With gratitude embrace the abundant gifts, talents, and resources He's given you to bear fruit for His Kingdom.

And discover how His overflow in you will manifest to those around you.

For Reflection and Regeneration

1. From the vision, how is the cave comparable to your soul?

2. Can you relate to any of the other "Cave Scenarios?" If so, how?

3. Give examples of gems in your life.
   a. What makes them beautiful and precious?
   b. What makes them abundant?

4. How can you bring the gems in your life into the lives of those around you?

5. As you go forth with the Holy Spirit and invest all of who you are in His Kingdom, what fruit are you hoping to bear?

6. How will connecting with Jesus regularly cause you to overflow with Him?

PEGGYANN POSS

A Fully Whelmed Life Scars Testimony

The words of a song come to mind, written and sung by a popular group, I AM THEY.

The song is titled SCARS. The lyrics go like this:

Waking up to a new sunrise
Looking back from the other side
I can see now with open eyes
Darkest water and deepest pain
I wouldn't trade it for anything
'Cause my brokenness brought me to you
And these wounds are a story you'll use
So I'm thankful for the scars
'Cause without them I wouldn't know your heart
And I know they'll always tell of who you are
So Forever I am thankful for the scars.

Now I'm sending in confidence
With the strength of your faithfulness
And I'm not who I was before
No I don't have to fear anymore

So I'm thankful for the scars
'Cause without them I wouldn't know your heart
And I know they'll always tell of who you are
So forever I am thankful for the scars

I can see, I can see
How you delivered me
In your hands, in your feet
I found my victory

I got off to a rough start in life by being born two months premature. I weighed 3 pounds and was in an incubator and kept in isolation for many months. Because of my underdeveloped lungs and poor immune system, I was labeled as "failure to thrive." In other words, they didn't expect me to live.

But I did.

From that very first day of life though, I struggled with physical health issues as well as emotional health issues. Because of my small size and being so underweight, I was kept alive on sugar water. This method of nourishment helped save my life, but it also created an addiction. By the age of three, I was on my way to obesity. At 18 I weighed 250 pounds, and by the time I was 40, I had reached 500 pounds. I suffered horrible teasing, bullying and prejudice at the hands of both children my age and adults. Depression and suicidal ideation clung to me like a wet blanket. I regularly felt isolated and "different" from those around me. Desperation seemed to hover over me. Not only that, but in addition to living in a fat, cumbersome body, my poor immune system left me open to illness after illness, diabetes, kidney failure, Charcot foot, arthritis, hypothyroidism, and hyperkalemia, and four bouts with cancer left me wondering if God just hated me. Why else would He allow so many awful things to happen to one person?

I became a Christian while in high school. For the first time in my life, I actually felt like I had a real friend. Yet, other circumstances in my life prevented me from trusting Him fully. Whenever I would land in the hospital, or yet another illness would raise its ugly head, I would rage at God. Yes, I prayed. But it felt like my prayers hit a ceiling, and I wondered if I really was his child and if he really did care about me. One minute I would trust God; the next, I would be filled with doubt, fear, and anger. The Bible taught me that my Heavenly Father loved me, but most often, my feelings convinced me that my circumstances were truthful and that God's word was not. Somehow I could not seem to square my circumstances with what the Bible said about who God was, nor with who it said I was.

Inside I knew that the "discrepancy" I felt had to be a lie within me, not in God. I knew that if my circumstances/life experience did not measure up to God's word, there had to be a problem with me.

Throughout my life I related better with animals than with people. In the last 20 years God blessed me with the privilege of owning several special critters. One in particular, a rescued Italian Greyhound named Enzo, captured my heart like none other. Having lost several children as well as having been rendered sterile from chemotherapy, this little guy became my "surrogate" child.

One particular day I was holding him in my arms like a baby when I realized the love I had for him was deeper than any love I had ever experienced before. As I held him in my arms, I heard the Holy Spirit speak the Father's words to me: "You know how much you love Enzo?" "I love YOU infinitely more than you love this little dog. I died for you. I gave everything for you. You are MINE. Trust ME. Trust the purpose I have in this life for you." That Holy Spirit conversation changed my life. I began to believe Him.

About a year after that incident, Enzo passed away. His passing broke me. I grieved in a way I never had before. Yet, even in the midst of feeling despair and loss, and even in the midst of yet another battle with depression, I knew something had changed. For the first time, I did not blame God or get angry at him. I did not feel guilty for experiencing this devastating loss deeply. In some ways, I felt inconsolable. Yet, I saw Jesus for who He was and Is, my Savior, the one who gives and the one who takes away.

It was like all the years of anger and fist shaking melted away. And what was left were scars. The isolation and loneliness of my childhood, the unfairness and agony of past and current health problems, and the deep sense of grief I had over losing Enzo came to rest at the feet of Jesus.

I realized all the pain, brokenness, and wounds of my past had a reason. Without these scars, I wouldn't know HIS heart. I wouldn't know His faithfulness. And I wouldn't know the victory of BEING HIS, in every circumstance.

I also came to a realization that Father God had a special calling on my life.

God has given me the privilege of going through so many difficulties in this life so that I can come alongside others who are hurting.

He has given me the privilege of coming alongside so that I can help bind up the broken hearted. I can share in and help carry the grief and pain others are experiencing.

I can say with humbleness "I've been there." And so has Jesus.

He has shown HIMSELF to me as the Lover of My Soul. I am His Beloved.

And I am thankful for the scars.

CHAPTER TWELVE

I-D-E-A-S

There are times I *think* I'm managing stress when suddenly I spew forth a hard-and-fast synopsis of everything that's on my mind, usually to an unsuspecting victim. (Uggh. It's that "verbal vomit" again, but on a smaller scale.) If it all gushes out spontaneously like that am I really "managing" it?

I did that to one of our church's pastors recently. We happened to pass each other in the stairway after I finished a meeting. All he said was, "Hi Lisa, how are you?" and gave me a friendly smile. For the next 60 seconds verbage shot from my mouth like pent-up fizz from a freshly opened soda can. I ended our (one-sided) conversation with, "Well, I better get going so I can start packing and catch my flight!"

What was whelming from within me in that moment? It was not a surge of love, joy and peace. Obviously I had some unfinished emotional business in my soul that needed resolving, regardless of the Presence of the Lord in my inner spirit. That wonderfully patient pastor provided an outlet for me to safely unload and scamper off.

I got in the car and thought, *What was that? What am I feeling?* I realized no matter how much I trust the Lord and have deep inner peace, any undealt-with emotions will lurk under the surface, looking for a crack to reveal pent-up unhealthy thinking.

IDEAS HAVE CONSEQUENCES

In 1948, author Richard M. Weaver wrote a book called "Ideas Have Consequences," which proved to be a controversial text regarding social order, individual rights, the acceptance of absolute reality, and the notion that ideas, like actions, have consequences. Our thoughts bear huge consequences in our lives because they trigger our feelings, which in turn inspire our actions, which result in consequences.

We get to choose what dictates our thoughts.

And do not be conformed to this world, but be transformed by the renewing of your mind, so that you may prove what the will of God is, that which is good and acceptable and perfect. Romans 12:2

Ideas have consequences, so if we are told in the Word of God to be transformed by the renewing of our mind, it follows that we get to work together with the Holy Spirit to make that happen, and consequently to produce results that bear fruit for His Kingdom.

It's a lot like choosing to make declarations of Christ's victory rather than declarations of defeat.

Our words stem from our thinking. Our words have consequences because our ideas have consequences. So when we become aware of our thinking, we get to discern whether it is setting itself up *against* the knowledge of God or *for* the knowledge of God.

We demolish arguments and every pretension that sets itself up against the knowledge of God, and we take captive every thought to make it obedient to Christ. 2 Corinthians 10:5

Recall the statement in the first chapter, "You choose your overwhelm." When we experience overwhelm, we may be feeling anxious, fearful, nervous, inept, burdened... the list goes on. These feelings stem from how we are *thinking* about our circumstances. Whether or not our circumstances are within our control, what we think about them determines whether we are setting ourselves up *for* or *against* the knowledge of God.

I-D-E-A-S

Let's use the acronym "IDEAS" as a tool for taking our thoughts captive and being transformed by the renewing of our mind.

I = **Identify** the feeling.

In a given circumstance, decide how you feel about it using one descriptive word. For example, when I got into my car after venting to my pastor, I was feeling "pressed." Avoid words like "bad" or "yucky" because they're too general. Be as specific as you can.

D = **Discern** the thought behind the feeling.

Discern what you are thinking and state it simply. For example, when I examined my thinking behind my feeling "pressed," I discerned, "I can't get it all done and somebody's going to be disappointed."

E = **Engage** the Holy Spirit.

If you discern that your thinking is not Christ-like, ask for the mind of Christ in that situation.

For who has understood the mind of the Lord so as to instruct him? But we have the mind of Christ. 1 Corinthians 2:16

Give it to the Holy Spirit, and ask Him to renew your mind and replace your thinking.

My prayer might sound something like, *Lord, I'm sorry. I'm feeling "pressed" because my thinking is very self-focused. Please replace it with your mind and your heart. Since you are beyond time and you invented it, I know that whatever you have designed for me will be accomplished in Your time. And Father, the only Person I seek approval from is You. When I'm operating through Your Spirit, You'll never be disappointed in me.*

A = **Act** accordingly.

Take a deep breath as you reset your thoughts. Once I realized I was feeling pressed because I was afraid of not doing enough and disappointing others, I changed my thinking through engaging the Holy Spirit. My new thought was, "There's enough time to do what God has called me to and His love for me is unconditional." As I let that sink in, I could feel motivated rather than pressed. I could more easily choose joy in the midst of my whirlwind. Consequently, I could move with a sense of urgency without desperation.

S = **Surrender** the results.

When your thoughts become motivated from a place of love instead of a place of fear, you can surrender the results of the actions you take based on those thoughts. God is bigger than the results - regardless of how we perceive them. My mom once said, "When you do anything, have the attitude of 'I'll do my best and trust God with the rest.'" I repeat that phrase often.

When we surrender results to Jesus, He will do more than we ask or imagine, not necessarily *what* we ask or imagine.

Now to him who is able to do immeasurably more than all we ask or imagine, according to his power that is at work within us...
Ephesians 3:20

When we pray, we often ask the Lord to change the circumstances in our life. "Lord, my boss is so demanding. Can you soften his heart toward me so he treats me better or transfer him to another location?" Likewise, we tend to pray for the Lord to change our results in our life. "Lord, if you get me out of this monster debt I'll be better about managing my money from now on!" We don't like how we feel about our circumstances or results of our behavior so we ask God to change them for us.

But God's not a genie in a bottle. He didn't die on the cross and rise from the dead just so we can be rescued from situations that we consider overwhelming. Yes, of course He does answer prayers that change circumstances and results. However, in His goodness, He also knows that walking through the fire produces results within us - and therefore good fruit - if we let it. He doesn't *cause* our trials. Rather, He's walking us *through* them. In addition, the way we think, feel, and act while we're in the midst of the fire will resonate to those around us.

A BIBLICAL APPLICATION

The story of Hananiah, Mishael, and Azariah in the book of Daniel illustrates this quite literally. Sure, the "fiery furnace" makes for a great Sunday School story that most of us have heard since childhood. Yet if we lean in, we'll hear the profound message the Biblical account sends to those of us who are facing overwhelming circumstances.

The three Jews, promising young men from the tribe of Judah, were among the "best of the best" of the captives that were brought to Babylon to serve King Nebuchadnezzar in 598/597 BCE. He changed their names to Shadrach, Meshach, and Abednego, and commanded that they be trained for the good of Babylon at the king's disposal. Imagine their situation. Their home of Jerusalem was demolished and their families were either killed or captured for

Babylon. Their names were changed and they had no choice but to serve their new king in a new culture with a new identity.

Sounds overwhelming.

However, the Lord blessed these young men and their faithfulness to Him.

And in every matter of wisdom and understanding about which the king inquired of them, he found them ten times better than all the magicians and enchanters that were in all his kingdom. Daniel 1:20

King Nebuchadnezzar did not worship the God of Abraham, Isaac, and Jacob as these young men did. History records he erected many temples to foreign gods, and in the book of Daniel we read that he created an image of gold that was 60 cubits high (about 90 feet) and demanded that it be worshipped.

...when you hear the sound of the horn, pipe, lyre, trigon, harp, bagpipe, and every kind of music, you are to fall down and worship the golden image that King Nebuchadnezzar has set up. And whoever does not fall down and worship shall immediately be cast into a burning fiery furnace. Daniel 3:4-6

Ideas have consequences, King Nebuchadnezzar.

After learning that Shadrach, Meshach and Abednego refused to worship his idol, the king summoned them to give them another chance. These were his top men, after all. He reminds them of their fiery fate if they do not bow to his idol and then states, "Then what god will rescue you out of my hands?" (Daniel 3:15).

We read their response in Daniel 3:17-18.

"O Nebuchadnezzar, we have no need to answer you in this matter. If this be so, our God whom we serve is able to deliver us from the

*burning fiery furnace, and he will deliver us out of your hand, O
king. But if not, be it known to you, o king, that we will not serve
your gods or worship the golden image that you have set up."*

"Our God whom we serve." Here they are explicitly stating that
they serve God above serving the king. They worship the God of the
Jews, not the gods of King Nebuchadnezzar.

WHAT ARE THE I-D-E-A-S HERE?

I = **Identify** the feeling. The three young men obviously felt
courage. (The king, on the other hand, was feeling furious as we read
in verse 19.)

D = **Discern** the thought. They told the king exactly what they
were thinking: "Our God whom we serve is able... and we will
not worship the golden image..." (We read that "the king's face
was changed against Shadrach, Meshach, and Abednego" so we
can hypothesize he was thinking something like, "These men need
punishment! The whole world is watching and I refuse to look like
a fool!")

E = **Engage** the Holy Spirit. With this great faith on display for
the king and all his kingdom to witness, it is obvious these men have
engaged the Holy Spirit. In Daniel 2 we read that they had already
avoided persecution by the king for another matter. Their friend
Daniel had given them advice.

*He urged them to plead for mercy from the God of heaven... so
that he and his friends might not be executed with the rest of the
wise men of Babylon. Daniel 2:18*

The three Jews engaged their God in that instance, and they
avoided persecution. Here they have another opportunity to engage

the Holy Spirit in their situation. (With what spirit was the king engaged?)

A = **Act** accordingly. Shadrach, Meshach, and Abednego didn't respond with fight, flight, freeze, faint, fawn, or fatigue. They faced it.

(King Nebuchadnezzar's actions, in accordance with his feelings, were to heat the furnace seven times more than it was usually heated and order his men to bind Shadrach, Meshach, and Abednego in their cloaks, tunics, hats, and other garments.)

S = **Surrender** the results. The young captors' words were, "... he is able to deliver us... and he will... but if not..." (verses 17-18). They were trusting, expectant, and surrendered to the outcome. (The king's position on the matter was non-negotiable, regardless of the possible outcomes. He was not surrendered. He was stubborn about what he wanted the results of his decree to look like.)

THE CONSEQUENCES

One consequence for the king was that he would lose three of his best men. Perhaps he considered that as he watched them head to the furnace. Another consequence is that he also lost all of his "mighty men" who escorted Shadrack, Meshack, and Abednego to the overheated furnace (verses 20, 22). The heat was so overwhelming they died en route!

God did not rescue these three young men from the fire. Everyone watched them enter the furnace.

So these men, wearing their robes, trousers, turbans and other clothes, were bound and thrown into the blazing furnace. Daniel 3:21

Like Shadrach, Meshach, and Abednego, we are not always rescued from our circumstances.

And like Shadrach, Meshach, and Abednego, we are never alone in our circumstances.

> *Then King Nebuchadnezzar leaped to his feet in amazement and asked his advisers, "Weren't there three men that we tied up and threw into the fire?" They replied, "Certainly, Your Majesty." He said, "Look! I see four men walking around in the fire, unbound and unharmed, and the fourth looks like a son of the gods." Nebuchadnezzar then approached the opening of the blazing furnace and shouted, "Shadrach, Meshach and Abednego, servants of the Most High God, come out! Come here!"* Daniel 3:24-26

UNBOUND AND UNHARMED

If you're feeling overwhelmed, you are walking in the fire. Despite the overwhelming flames, you do not need to be in a state of "defeated overwhelm." (I do not get the impression from reading about Shadrack, Meshach, and Abednego they ever felt defeated in their overwhelming circumstance.) Instead, you can live in that place of peace, trust, and surrender, which only happens when you acknowledge and embrace the Lord's Presence in the fire with you. In this place of complete dependence and trust, here's what happens (see Daniel 3:26-27):

- The fire will not harm your body (Daniel 3:26-27).

  - *When you pass through the waters, I will be with you; and when you pass through the rivers, they will not sweep over you. When you walk through the fire, you will not be burned; the flames will not set you ablaze.* Isaiah 43:2

- Not a hair of your head will be singed (Daniel 3:27).

  - *You will be hated by all for my name's sake. But not a hair of your head will perish. By your endurance you will gain your lives.* Luke 21:17-19

- Your robe will not be scorched (Daniel 3:27).

  - *I delight greatly in the Lord; my soul rejoices in my God. For he has clothed me with garments of salvation and arrayed me in a robe of his righteousness.* Isaiah 61:10

- You will not even smell like smoke (Daniel 3:27).

  - *But thanks be to God, who always leads us in triumph in Christ, and manifests through us the sweet aroma of the knowledge of Him in every place. For we are a fragrance of Christ to God among those who are being saved and among those who are perishing;* 2 Corinthians 2:14-15

God is not like King Nebuchadnessar. He did not throw us into the fire. He's our Savior, He's our Deliverer, and He's walking through the fire with us.

Ideas have consequences. We can choose to become buried in our thoughts and feelings about our circumstances or we can choose to take our thoughts captive, engage with the Holy Spirit, and surrender the results of the actions we take that are based in Truth and Love.

For Reflection and Regeneration

1. Consider one specific situation in your life that you
   would consider a trial.
   a. The situation is a fact. Do not apply thoughts or
      feelings to it. Simply recognize the situation. (For
      example, *My best friend is not returning my calls.*)

2. Apply the IDEAS acronym to it. Write it for better clarity.
   a. I: Identify in one word how you feel about it.
      (Example: *hurt*)
   b. D: Discern in one simple phrase your thought behind
      that feeling. (Example: *She's either upset with me or
      doesn't care about me.*)
   c. E: Engage the Holy Spirit. Is your thinking coming
      from the Lord (based in Truth) or coming from
      the enemy (who wants to steal, kill, and destroy)?
      (Example: *Lord, I don't know why she's not calling me.
      If she's upset or doesn't care, Father, I give that to you
      and ask you to restore our relationship. If she's struggling
      with something on her end, Lord, give me grace and
      patience to allow her to work through it. Lord, I pray
      for her relationship with you, that she draws close to you
      during this time.*)
   d. A: Act accordingly. (Example: Create a new thought
      about the situation. *She's not calling me back because
      she's going through something right now, so I'll continue
      to pray for her.* Contact the friend and let her know
      you're thinking and praying for her and that you'll be
      there for her when she's ready to connect.)

e. S: Surrender the results. (Example: *I am available to love her, pray for her, and be there for her. I will give her space to work through this and trust that You are in it, Lord. Our friendship belongs to you. My feelings belong to you. I give it all to you and trust that because you already know the results here, you'll help me to accept and love her regardless of how I think it's supposed to look.*)

3. What could it look like to walk through a fire (an overwhelming circumstance) and not "smell like smoke" when you come out of the furnace? (In other words, what do you want to whelm from you after experiencing a trial?)

DUGAN SHERBONDY

A Fully Whelmed Agonized Father Testimony

(Excerpts from Dugan's online Facebook journal,
quoted with his blessing.)

Aug 23

Our (7-year-old) daughter Eva Love suffered a severe head injury today, which resulted in some significant brain trauma. She was rushed to the emergency room and right into surgery. The surgery went well but the next 72 hours of her recovery are vital. Please just pray.

Aug 26

We prayed for a miraculous or clear scan. Unfortunately that's not what came back. The results were very difficult to hear... After these past days of praying for the miraculous, hearing thousands of other prayers and visions and stories of hope, I was faithfully confident we'd see a miracle today. Instead, I felt like I was getting punched in the gut with phrases like "permanent brain damage" and "continued swelling" and "we'll keep her sedated for another week." ...God's timing is perfect. He is sovereign and in control. He is healing and taking care of Eva and has been quite literally since the moment she hit her head (we'll tell all the amazing stories of God presence and protection soon enough)... There is a God, it is not me. God knows, and that is enough.

Sep 4

Medically, the doctors are gently saying... tthe best we could hope for would be some eventual movement of her eyes and limbs...after a year of rehabilitation. They even looked us in the eyes and asked, based on their prediction of her future quality of life, if we'd like to keep her on life-support or not...

What the heck, God? ...I've never felt more like I need to sob and also smash everything I can touch than I do today. ...I'm out of prayers. I feel like I've been praying non-stop for 2 weeks straight and am running on fumes. I mean, Jesus simply spoke healing and life and authority over sickness and death once and people were healed or rose from the dead. Why is God taking so long in answering my prayers? ...I'm angry and empty and lost and a million miles past confused. But still trying to hold on to this:

"I waited patiently for the Lord to help me, and he turned to me and heard my cry. He lifted me out of the pit of despair, out of the mud and the mire. He set my feet on solid ground and steadied me as I walked along. He has given me a new song to sing, a hymn of praise to our God. Many will see what he has done and be amazed. They will put their trust in the Lord." - Psalm 40:1-3

Sep 10

There has been so, so, so, so much GOOD that has come out of the last two and a half weeks, that despite my pain or fear, it is undeniable that God has been present and showing His power in so many ways. So, right after I post this, I'm going to sit down and make a list of every single thing I have to be thankful to God for since the moment Eva hit her head.

Sep 12

I'll never forget a quote I heard years ago about this passage that said: "The problem with a living sacrifice is that it always has the option of crawling off the altar."

And the difficult part of this daily surrendering of Eva is I'm constantly battling taking her off the altar and keeping her all to myself to do things my way. But I'm learning how to worship God through my surrender and as I do, praying He reshapes the way I think and my faith and we see His will (which is good and pleasing and perfect) unfold. All I can do is just keep praying and believing and surrendering.

Sept 17

In addition to surrendering my daughter, I'm also now surrendering my expectations or desire to control what happens. It's amazing how much effort it's requiring to intentionally wait like this. It's like I have to take a thousand purposeful Sabbaths each day to ensure I'm quieting my spirit and casting my cares upon Jesus.

Sept 21

... I take comfort in the following truth: Hindsight is coming. There will be a day I look back and this all makes sense. A day when I'll see all that God was doing and see the wisdom and power and purpose in being stuck in the middle right now. It might be tomorrow or in 20 years (gosh, hopefully not that long), but that is coming and I know it...and I can hardly wait, but I will.

Oct 1

...It's been a daily discipline, painful at times, to practice surrendering Eva to God during a time when I want to hold her closer than I ever have before. As a dad, all I want to do is fix it and make her laugh, but God has made it clear again and again that He's got her, He's in control, He's sovereign, He's good, and He has a plan.

Oct 5

Today was a roller coaster. The distance to Eva's miraculous healing seems further.

...And in the midst of my stress and doubt and fear and hurt, I choose to remember who God is and what He has promised.

Oct 24

She's had a couple very rough days recently...

It is the most draining thing I've ever experienced. This can't be the end. This can't be the way God wants Eva to be for the rest of her life. I do not understand why God has not gotten her up yet.

And for whatever it's worth, I know all the things I would say to myself. "God's timing is perfect," "Even small progress is worth celebrating,"...I know them, I've heard them, I get it. But I'm still left wondering when God is going to heal Eva, while also thinking about living the rest of our lives with just a shell of our daughter. What now, Lord? Tomorrow I'm going to write about some things God is teaching me through Scripture, but for today, I needed to be real about how difficult this truly is at times.

Nov. 2

...The results of faith are amazing, but in the middle of faith, it's just super painful. However in spite of what I see in front of me, I'm still praying, still believing, still hoping. Desperately.

Nov 7

I came up with a new definition for faith today: Faith is like standing in a boxing ring with my hands tied behind my back, taking punch after punch...but still believing I will win the fight.

Dec 3

In the midst of all this, we have so many things and, more importantly, people to be thankful for. God has shown Himself to be ever present and faithful. The light at the end of the tunnel is coming but even in the middle of the darkness, it is well.

Dec 15

Linds and I were told by one of Eva's doctors this past week that they are all "mildly shocked" that Eva is alive and doing as well as she is. So clearly, God is present and healing. And just because He isn't doing it in the way/timing I'd like, doesn't mean He isn't.

Dec 23

I've realized recently that I've been focusing a lot more on the healing vs. the Healer. ...many of my prayers are more "to" God and less with Him. Plus with our lives getting adjusted to a new normal with us all being home, it's easy to go through my day and not really seek God (aside from asking Him to heal Eva). So, I've started taking time each day to read Scripture with Eva and pray, making sure to take time to listen to God, not just talk at Him.

God continues to give me a sense that she is already healed and that it's simply "not yet" time for her to get up. In the meantime, I'm so grateful to have my whole family together. I'm so glad to be able to hang out with and kiss my girl throughout the day. Of course there are difficult moments of pain and deep uncertainty, but I'm choosing to have a heart of gratitude and worship towards our great God and my Heavenly Father.

Dec 28

Linds said to me today: "It's so exhausting having this excruciating hope." And yet...we still have hope. All the hopes. ...That's all I got left. Hope, hope, hope. God's not done. He's still working and doing so much good. And He is going to heal His daughter soon. Until then, we just wait, love our girl, and hope all the hope we can muster.

Jan 1

...And we still believe healing is coming. The further away we get from Eva's accident, the more difficult it is to remain confident in that belief, but we can't stop, won't stop believing and praying. I fully understand that God is not in a hurry, that He is patient, that He is working and moving and doing so many good things, but every day that goes by and Eva isn't healed yet just makes me wonder why it's taking so long. Am I praying incorrectly? Am I doing something that's preventing healing or not doing something to release it? Is God just not done yet? What's He waiting for?

Jan 7

Waiting is something our culture seems to be doing everything it can to eliminate, and yet God seems to teach that waiting is just fine. I don't know the ending to Eva's story. I know the ending that I'm praying and believing for, but I don't know for sure. Nor do I know how long we'll have to wait before that ending. So for now, I wait. And wait. And wait. And then something else...oh yea, wait.

> *...And from everything I've studied in Scripture, waiting means a few things: God is with me (Micah 7:7), God will bless me (Lamentations 3:25), and God is working in the waiting (Lamentations 29:11-13).*

> *Simeon waited, Saul waited, even Jesus waited for God to move. I hate it, but I'm slowly beginning to embrace that I need to wait. And that waiting is okay.*

> *"May you be strengthened with all power, according to his glorious might, for all endurance and patience with joy..." Colossians 1:11*

CHAPTER THIRTEEN

Wrapping Up in love

My maternal grandmother reminds me of Jesus every time I think of her. She's with Him now, being wrapped in His love the way she wrapped me (and everyone she knew) in hers while she was on earth.

Grandma's sweet, giggly demeanor was infectious and her Norwegian accent was as thick as her middle. Growing up, we had a framed cross-stitch craft on the wall that said, "If Mother Says No Ask Grandmother." So accurate. She had an abundance of yesses simply because she believed the best about everyone and with that, brought out the best in everyone.

As an only child experiencing my parents' divorce around age 4, I didn't know what "overwhelm" meant and I didn't understand what was happening. I simply sensed the turmoil in my circumstances. I couldn't have realized at the time how much Grandma's love overflowed onto me in the midst of that season and beyond.

My favorite moments with Grandma at that time were spent on a simple black leather chair in her living room. I would crawl onto grandma's ample lap and nestle in as she wrapped her loving arms around me. The chair wasn't a rocker, but Grandma rocked anyway, humming a peaceful, repetitive tune in sync with her movements.

There was nothing more soothing than the melodious vibration of her humming while we rocked in that chair. Drifting to sleep in her cushiony lap was like being wrapped in the arms of Jesus: comforting, strong, secure, connected, peaceful, and filled with so much love.

Once satiated, I would slide off Grandma's lap fully whelmed with her love, ready for whatever my next moment held, knowing she'd be ready to wrap me in another "love fix" when I needed it.

Just like Jesus.

I knew Grandma valued those times too. She had an abundant supply of love and had a special relationship with all her kids and grandkids. She loved us all like we were her favorite.

Just like Jesus.

AN UNUSUAL TRIBUTE

Grandma was buried several years ago in a cemetery behind a white steepled church perched on a hill overlooking miles of rolling farmland. Our grieving family gathered for her interment and the pastor spoke his words of comfort and committal. When there was nothing left to be said, we all stood tearfully gazing at the casket, wallowing in the empty silence of our great loss.

As if on cue, an enormous buzzing cloud of bees swarmed directly over us like a military squadron on a mission. I've never seen anything like it before or since. I stood there dumbfounded. The timing and magnitude of it were surreal and far too coincidental to be coincidental.

In her lifetime, Grandma had seen more hardship and suffered more loss than most of us. She had more reasons for defeated overwhelm than I could ever know. Yet she overflowed pure love. Her hope-filled surrender to her Savior whelmed from the inside out. Because she regularly spent time in His Presence, His Presence flowed from her and soaked the people around her.

On the day she was buried, the Lord seemed to use the giant swarm of bees to honor to this woman who loved so well through all of her life's joys *and* tribulations. The insects' resonating purr reminds me of Grandma's humming as she rocked me in that black chair so many years ago. It was strong and soothing, peaceful and powerful; almost supernatural. What a fitting tribute.

What does it look like to shift from overwhelm to overflow? What does it mean to be fully whelmed? It looks like my Grandma. It looks like peace, hope, and love that radiates from within. It means loving Jesus and people more than fearing my circumstances. It means even when my circumstances are not okay, *I'm* okay because I'm surrendered to the One Who wraps me in His arms until I'm whelming with Him.

PERSPECTIVES THAT SHIFT US FROM OVERWHELM TO OVERFLOW

Let's review the journey we've been on within the pages of this book.

Chapter 1: Overwhelming circumstances happen. You get to choose whether your overwhelm is defeated (hopeless) or surrendered (trusting that the Lord knows your circumstances, that He is ultimately good, and that nothing can separate you from His love).

Chapter 2: If you know Jesus as your Savior, you are a saint at your core (in your spirit). You get to choose if you're going to let your circumstances (re)define you or if the Holy Spirit Who abides in you defines you. (You can live from the outside in or from the inside out.)

Chapter 3: To be whelmed is to experience the Holy Spirit surging from within you regardless of the overwhelm that may be happening around you. You can whelm so much with Him and His love that it overflows.

Chapter 4: Fear and overwhelm go hand in hand. When you simply face it (acknowledging what IS) instead of fighting it, ignoring it, or hiding from it, you surrender your false sense of control over it so Jesus can walk you through it.

Chapter 5: When in the midst of overwhelming circumstances, rather than exhausting yourself from performing *for* Jesus, take His hand and walk *with* Him. Release your expectations and be ready to take yourself and the Lord out of the box (of how life is "supposed" to look) so you can fly with Him. He can do more than you can ask or imagine.

Chapter 6: Creating yokes for yourself and telling Jesus to join them and bless them is exhausting. Step into His yoke and let Him be the lead oxen. His burden is easy and His yoke is light. The shorter your flight distance from the Father, the easier it is to have the freedom to say no to self-made yokes and the freedom to say yes to the Lord's.

Chapter 7: The root cause of defeated overwhelm is a scarcity mentality. Because God is abundant, He can bless you abundantly in all things at all times, causing you to abound (overflow) in every good work. (See 2 Corinthians 9:8.)

Chapter 8: Savor Jesus. Don't allow your relationship to become a "necessary chore" just because you know it's good for you. Cramming time with Him when the going gets tough is not going to prevent overwhelm. *Be with* Jesus so you can *do with* Jesus.

Chapter 9: When the rubber hits the road, you find out what you've really surrendered. When you surrender every aspect of your life to Him, you are less likely to experience defeated overwhelm when any area undergoes a trial because you recognize everything is in His hands already.

Chapter 10: Words have power. We can use them to declare perpetual defeat or to declare the goodness of God and the hope we have in Him. When your emotions are triggered, embrace being fully human in expressing them while allowing the Holy Spirit to be your go-to Comforter and your filter.

Chapter 11: When Jesus is on your throne, the gifts, talents, and resources He's given you are abundant and meant to bear fruit for God's Kingdom. They are proportionate to your capacity to use them and their blessings will abound for you and others when you are consistently in communion with Jesus.

Chapter 12: Ideas have consequences. We can take our thoughts captive in any situation by identifying our feeling about it, discerning the thought that triggered the feeling, engaging the Holy Spirit, acting accordingly, and surrendering the results.

Fully Whelmed Testimonies: Be encouraged by stories of people who have experienced overwhelm and how they came to a place of overflow. If God can whelm in them He can whelm in you too.

A FINAL LOVING WRAP-UP

I've been praying for you while writing this book: that you will receive God's overwhelming love for you and that you will allow it to fill you so that it whelms within you and overflows.

He's bigger than any circumstance you're facing. He's *with* you in it. Wrap up your reading of this book by wrapping up in the Father's extravagant love for you. Crawl onto Jesus's lap. Soak in His Presence.

And be fully whelmed.

May the God of hope fill you with all joy and peace as you trust in him, so that you may overflow with hope by the power of the Holy Spirit. Romans 15:13

Bibliographic References

Chapter 3

1. Wickman, Kase. "We Solved the Most Enduring Mystery." *MTV. com.* May 6, 2016. February 2020.

2. "US Dictionary." *Lexico.com.* Oxford. February 2020.

Chapter 4

1. Heaney, Katie. "I'm So Tired: When Stress Makes You Fall Asleep." *TheCut.com.* July 11, 2017. February 2020.

Chapter 6

1. Conroy, Drew. "Tillers' TechGuide: Advanced Training Techniques for Oxen." Tillers International. 1995.

2. "Training New Oxen." lhf.org/2015/01/training-new-oxen. *Living History Farms.* February 2020.

Chapter 7

1. "Vocabulary.com Dictionary." Vocabulary.com. February 2020.

Chapter 12

1. Weaver, Richard M. *Ideas Have Consequences.* University of Chicago Press. 1948, 2013.

About the Author

Lisa Dettinger is a Christian life coach, speaker, author, teacher, curriculum writer, and e-course creator who loves facilitating "aha" moments. She combines her love for Jesus, her experience working with adults and children, and her continuing education to promote spiritual, mental, and emotional freedom through connecting with God and people. She and her husband Travis have been married since 1993 and live near Madison, Wisconsin, where they are active in their thriving church. They've raised and educated three amazing children who are now blazing their own inspiring paths in life. When she's not working on her "next big project," Lisa enjoys life and ministry with Travis, working out, coffee shop dates with friends, reading, and travelling.

Lisa's motto: "To live IS Christ" (Phil. 1:21). She is fully whelmed.

Made in the USA
Columbia, SC
21 February 2020